# Witnesses
of
Synodality

# Witnesses of Synodality

## Good Practices and Experiences

EDITED BY
**Jos Moons, SJ**

FOREWORD BY
**Austen Ivereigh**

Paulist Press
New York / Mahwah, NJ

Scripture quotations are from New Revised Standard Version Bible: Catholic Edition, copyright © 1989, 1993 National Council of the Churches of Christ in the United States of America. Used by permission. All rights reserved worldwide.

Cover image by nikolai2 / Depositphotos.com
Cover design by Joe Gallagher
Book design by Lynn Else

Copyright © 2024 by Jos Moons, SJ

All rights reserved. No part of this publication may be reproduced, stored in a retrieval system, or transmitted in any form or by any means, electronic, mechanical, photocopying, recording, scanning, or otherwise, without either the prior written permission of the Publisher, or authorization through payment of the appropriate per-copy fee to the Copyright Clearance Center, Inc., www.copyright.com. Requests to the Publisher for permission should be addressed to the Permissions Department, Paulist Press, permissions@paulistpress.com.

Library of Congress Cataloging-in-Publication Data
Names: Moons, Jos, 1980– editor.
Title: Witnesses of synodality: good practices and experiences / edited by Jos Moons, SJ.
Description: New York; Mahwah, NJ : Paulist Press, [2024] | Summary: "This book provides eleven examples of Synodality operating at different levels and areas of the church"—Provided by publisher.
Identifiers: LCCN 2023049402 (print) | LCCN 2023049403 (ebook) | ISBN 9780809156962 (paperback) | ISBN 9780809188598 (ebook)
Subjects: LCSH: Councils and synods.
Classification: LCC BV710 .W58 2024 (print) | LCC BV710 (ebook) | DDC 262/.52—dc23/eng/20240409
LC record available at https://lccn.loc.gov/2023049402
LC ebook record available at https://lccn.loc.gov/2023049403

ISBN 978-0-8091-5696-2 (paperback)
ISBN 978-0-8091-8859-8 (e-book)

Published by Paulist Press
997 Macarthur Boulevard
Mahwah, NJ 07430
www.paulistpress.com

Printed and bound in the
United States of America

Dedication

*To Pope Francis.*
*In thanksgiving to God*
*for his courage, love, and spiritual wisdom.*

# Contents

Foreword: Embracing Synodal Conversion
 by *Austen Ivereigh* .................................................................. ix

Introduction ............................................................................... xv

1. Synodal Wisdom from the Rule of Benedict ......................... 1
   Rebekka Willekes, OCSO

2. Dominican Gifts for a Synodal Church ............................... 14
   Stefan Mangnus, OP

3. A Franciscan Approach to Synodality ................................. 27
   Noel Muscat, OFM

4. An Ursuline Perspective of Synodality ................................ 39
   Laure Blanchon, OSU, and Armida Veglio, OSU

5. Common Discernment and the Founding
   of the Jesuits ........................................................................ 53
   Jos Moons, SJ

6. Community Discernment amid Violence:
   The Monks of Tibhirine ....................................................... 65
   Marie-Dominique Minassian

7. A Parish Experience of Synodality: Holy Trinity
   Catholic Church, Georgetown ............................................ 79
   Brian Flanagan

8. A Diocesan Experience of Synodality: San Diego ............. 92
   John E. Hurley, CSP

## Contents

9. Australia's Plenary Council .................................................. 105
   *Richard Lennan*

10. Synodality through an African Lens:
    Palaver and Ubuntu ........................................................ 118
    *Anne Arabome, sss*

11. Synodality in a Continental Perspective:
    Latin America and the Caribbean................................... 131
    *Birgit Weiler, mms*

About the Contributors ...........................................................145

# Foreword
## Embracing Synodal Conversion

The synodal conversion of the Catholic Church now underway is the most significant shift in its internal culture in modern times. It will be seen in the future as Pope Francis's most important reform. The three-year synod on synodality process (2021–24), involving the whole people of God and the church at every level—parish, diocese, country, continent, universal—is one vast act of self-transcendence, opening the church as an institution to the Spirit and the people, and to the Spirit *in* the people. It is a conversion in the authentic sense of that word, for it demands that we take seriously—and enable, in our church practices and structures—Jesus's promise that he would send his Spirit, and the Spirit would lead the church into the truth.

Because it is a conversion, it is challenging; it involves the shedding of one way of thinking and operating and adopting another, closer to the gospel. Like all profound changes, it needs to be lived to be properly understood. It is known by experience rather than by reading manuals of ecclesiology. The iconic example remains the experience of the disciples in chapter 15 of the Acts of the Apostles: divided and unsure, they sought the guidance of the Spirit through an intensive sharing of experiences in which all were involved. The breakthrough there—a surprise of the Spirit—freed the early church to sow the seeds of the gospel in every culture.

## Witnesses of Synodality

Perhaps the most encouraging part of the early, diocesan phase of the synod on synodality was to see how quickly people took to it, recognizing in the prayerful listening method of "Conversation in the Spirit" something authentically "ours." This recognition by the people of God of synodality as a properly ecclesial way of proceeding is itself a sign of the Spirit, for all true reform in the church, as Yves Congar reminds us, is a recovery of something intrinsic or essential that has become sidelined or ignored over time. In calling, now, for the church to recover its first-millennium way of proceeding, in ways appropriate to our times, Pope Francis is not asking us to take on something from the outside but to be more truly faithful to the Catholic tradition: to depend not on our own resources but the power of grace.

The readable chapters that follow explain how synodality works now, in practice, in the church, at the most varied of levels and in the greatest variety of circumstances. And they offer reflections on those experiences—tools, lessons, fruits—that are pertinent to the synodal conversion. If, at that first synodal meeting in Acts 15—the Council of Jerusalem as it was later known—were the first witnesses of synodality, in the pages that follow are some of their modern-day successors, taking those same vital elements and applying them to decision-making and discernment.

In one famous example, French Trappist monks decide eventually to stay in Algeria to face certain martyrdom. In another, the Ursuline sisters in a small rural town decide to buy a second car. In both cases, synodality bears the same fruit: those involved learn to live in fruitful tension, grow together, and prayerfully reach a consensus around what is, as far as they can tell, God's will. Marie-Dominique Minassian draws the lesson from the Tibhirine martyrs that the kind of "integral listening" they did is "crucial for any parish, community, or group." Only by listening to one another, to Scripture, and to the events and circumstances we are faced with—in momentous moments,

## Foreword

but also in small, everyday decisions—in openness, mutual interdependence, and availability to the action of the Spirit, can we become living witnesses to the gospel in our time, and our parishes and apostolic bodies beacons of communion, mission, and participation.

This is what Francis is asking the church to embrace, at every level. And it is no accident that making that call is a Jesuit pope from the church in Latin America, which, as Birgit Weiler shows, has been on a decades-long journey of synodal deepening. The best teacher of synodality is the experience of it.

Hence the important place in this volume of the religious orders, for they have long preserved or reinvigorated the habits and practices of early church synodality, after the postmedieval diocesan church abandoned them in favor of more worldly forms of sovereignty. The chapters here on and by Benedictines, Dominicans, Franciscans, Jesuits, and Ursulines are packed with deep wisdom and fascinating insights from their own experiences, past and present. Here we learn what it means to be humble, obedient, and receptive in community deliberations; the importance of patience and resisting the temptation to resolve the tensions too soon; and what it means to exercise authority in synodal processes. They show that discernment is not easy; there is never absolute certainty about God's will, even if the signs seem plentiful. Yet, as Rebekka Willekes says, "the Spirit also works through our wrong decisions," leading the community toward its goal sometimes via a diversion.

In each case, one constant lesson is making the consultation broad and deep. Give it time and make space for it. In Africa, the traditional "palaver" experience of communal dialogue is "often imagined as a dialogical experience that happens under a tree," says Anne Arabome. Keep it open, as if under a tree on a plain; don't shut out the voices where the Spirit may be speaking in the least likely spaces. For "there is no border that this movement of the Spirit does not feel compelled to cross, to

# Witnesses of Synodality

draw all into its dynamism," as the *Instrumentum Laboris* for the 2023 Synod of Bishops puts it.

"What should we do when a conversation gets stuck?" asks Stefan Mangnus. His answer: "Do not force a solution, but look for ways to initiate a process." This is where all synodality starts: in an acceptance of our incapacity to resolve our differences through debate or power. Synodality is a method, says Jos Moons, of moving forward in disagreement, converting it into discernment, thus allowing the Spirit to break us out of the confines of our thinking and reveal to us a new (and always bigger and more beautiful) horizon. Consider the crisis moment in July 2022, recounted here by Richard Lennan, when the Australian Plenary Council deliberations ran into a divisive impasse over the issue of women's participation in ministry and leadership. Instead of pressing on, dividing the assembly into opposing camps, they stopped the proceedings and, yes, created a process. After deep listening and prayer, consensus was created; the motions were clarified and strengthened. The impasse became a source of grace and growth.

And in dioceses and parishes? This is a journey most are just beginning. But here are two examples from the United States. In San Diego, Cardinal Robert McElroy has twice used diocesan synods to embrace the fruits of Rome synods: to receive *Amoris Laetitia* in 2016 and *Christus Vivit* in 2018. The first led to a makeover in the way San Diego nurtures marriages and accompanies the unmarried; the second led to programs to bolster the active participation of young people in the life and mission of the diocese. In a big Jesuit parish in Washington, DC, meanwhile, they knew that synodal listening is to be followed by concrete action: as Brian Flanagan documents, hearing women's desire for ministry led to new ways of proclaiming the gospel.

Synodality is not democracy but something well upstream of it. Reading these chapters, superbly compiled and edited by Jos Moons, SJ, you realize just how much a healthy democracy depends on the virtues and practices of synodality. This is a time

## Foreword

when democracies are wobbling, voters shut themselves away in warring camps, dialogue descends into parallel monologues, and the creation of consensus to deal with common challenges seems ever less likely. Yet, just at this moment, the Spirit is calling the world's oldest, most global institution—at a moment where it, too, is unsure, and its conversations also stuck—to reach back into its own tradition to find an underground stream of grace. Pope Francis likes to quote the poet Friedrich Hölderlin: "there, where the danger is, grows the saving power." Here, where the danger of division and paralysis is, Catholics are rediscovering the ancient saving art of growing together through deep mutual, receptive listening.

This is a journey of profound conversion now for the church. But not so long from now, its harvest will be reaped by humanity.

*Austen Ivereigh*

# Introduction

This book encourages and equips those of good will who want to move forward with synodality. First, it hopes to warm their hearts by sharing testimonies from within the Roman Catholic Church's very own tradition. Synodal types of governing are already being practiced, and clearly the experience has been positive. Such models are as old as the Rule of Benedict, which goes back to the sixth century, and has even older roots. Inclusive and participative decision taking has deep cultural roots, for example, in the African "palaver" tradition. The monks of Tibhirine have proven that taking decisions together is possible and helpful even in difficult and disturbing circumstances, such as the life-threatening context of Algeria. Interestingly, synodal practices exist in shapes and forms as varied as the democratic tradition of the Dominicans and the tradition of discernment of the Jesuits. And finally, the collaboration at the level of the Latin American Church (CELAM), the Australian Church's Plenary Synod, or the Diocese of San Diego's diocesan synods prove that synodal ways of proceeding are not the exclusive possession of religious congregations and orders.

Second, the book also has a more practical objective. A group of experts highlight eleven good practices, each of which provides tools for synodality that one may safely "try at home." These attitudes, practices, or procedures range from trust in the Holy Spirit and a prayerful attitude to cultivating a culture of conversation, bearing with one another's different views, bringing in professional expertise, patience, and so on.

## Witnesses of Synodality

# Synodality as a Practical Challenge

The focus of this book is on the *practice* of synodality. Pope Francis and the Secretariat for the Synod like to speak about synodality as "a journey" (*cammino*), a "dynamism" (*dinamismo*), a "style," and "walking together." While not denying that synodality comes with a set of theoretical ideas about the church—such as the priority of the people of God, the complementarity between the magisterium and the *sensus fidei*, and so on—they highlight the ways of behaving that it supposes. The key words are by now well-known but remain a challenge when it comes to putting them into practice: discernment, openness, listening, prayer, inclusion, participation, transparency, and so on.

It is indeed my deep conviction that synodality comes with both theoretical and practical challenges and that the latter are as difficult as the former. Learning new habits always is. Those who wield the sword of "orthodoxy" to silence people with different understandings of the Catholic faith must learn to tolerate these differences. Those who are more progressive need a similar magnanimity, resisting the temptation to qualify those with different convictions as "backward." Those who are "silent" and usually keep their opinions to themselves must learn to share their views with confidence. All of us must learn to respect one another without labeling our sisters and brothers as old-fashioned, conservative, traditionalist, liberal, progressive, silly, or stupid.

This, however, is the first step. Once we manage to engage in a *meaningful conversation* with people who hold different views, the still greater challenge to *learn* from one another awaits us. Synodality is about hearing the Spirit's voice speaking to the church through our brothers and sisters. It is, therefore, a spiritual undertaking. The key question is, where in our conversations are we sensing the Spirit's gentle breeze? The answer requires a fundamental openness and a willingness to change. Pope Francis has

## Introduction

introduced the notion of "overflow": the experience that someone, something, breaks open our narrow human minds to the greater horizon of God's grace. Yet, how does one encounter what Francis calls "the newness of the Spirit" or "the surprises of the Spirit"?

## The Church as a Novice

This process of learning new habits could be profitably compared to a novitiate. The word *novice* means both "inexperienced" and "a person at the early stage of formation into the religious life." Clearly, theory is part of overcoming one's lack of experience. For example, as an inexperienced, aspiring Jesuit novice, I had to read the Constitutions, the history of the Society of Jesus, the life of Ignatius, books on spiritual discernment, and so on. But we spent much more time on practical learning in its various forms: living community life (with its ups and downs), carrying out humble tasks in the house (the "indoor works" and "outdoor works"), serving the needy in our Thursday morning apostolate with the homeless or the elderly, being exposed to new contexts during a six-week school placement and a six-week pilgrimage (without money!), all while developing a reflective and contemplative prayer in all those varying contexts. Apparently, progressing in the art of being a Jesuit depended more on practice than on theory.

If the church is indeed like an inexperienced novice who is just beginning its formation in a more inclusive and participative synodal lifestyle, the church's novitiate, too, should involve both theory and practice.

That such practical learning is much needed is obvious. Examples of the church's poor synodal skills abound. For instance, I remember a formation session on growing in synodality with a group of parishes. After listening to the issues and

## Witnesses of Synodality

how the group wanted to proceed, I suggested that, instead of sharing the solution with the parishioners, they could also share the problems. In that way, they would not be operating from the top down, instructing how problems were to be solved, but in a collaborative manner. Who knows, the parishioners might contribute good ideas! And, if not, they would at least have been included in the process from knowing the problems to finding the solutions. It speaks volumes that something as simple as sharing the problem was a revelation: we are not used to an inclusive and participative way of being church.

Yet, various decisions by the Secretariat for the Synod show that the church is making progress in practicing synodality. The Secretariat has redesigned the process of the Synod 2021–2024 more than once. For example, the diocesan listening phase was prolonged when bishops complained that the proposed time schedule was too tight. Moreover, the Secretariat later split the concluding synod into two sessions so that the synod now ends in 2024. Instead of rushing to a close, the Secretariat wanted to give the bishops (and the whole church) ample time for discernment. Furthermore, it has felt that laypeople needed more involvement, which led to lay participants being invited to the official meetings during the second, "continental" phase. Similarly, it also made sense to invite laypeople to participate in the 2023 Synod of Bishops and to give them voting rights. Finally, it was decided that the synod would take place in the Paul VI *aula* (and not in the usual synod *aula*), thus allowing for roundtable conversations. In all these cases, the Secretariat felt that another approach would better facilitate the practice of synodality. Problems or hindrances were not solved by theoretical clarity but by practical adaptations.

Highlighting one more aspect of the novitiate life helps demonstrate how this book may be useful for the church's learning process. Novices are usually supposed to learn from inspiring and instructive brothers and sisters, past and present, whose

Introduction

examples they can safely imitate. For example, in my novitiate, we had to prepare brief homilies on the Jesuit saints commemorated on the liturgical calendar. Moreover, we met various Jesuits in active ministry, some of whom were great examples of courage and commitment, such as the Jesuits working for reconciliation in Northern Ireland, or a pioneering Jesuit who is one of the founders of Pray As You Go. So, too, for the church in its synodal novitiate. This book follows the same logic by presenting eleven edifying and inspiring examples of "sisters" and "brothers" for us to imitate.

## Theological Foundations for Practice

While the book focuses on the practice of synodality, practice always supposes and "incarnates" theory. Just as prayer and faith determine one another—*lex orandi, lex credendi*—so do theory and practice. (One could say: *lex credendi, lex vivendi*.) By way of justification, let me point out some theoretical foundations that support a practice-focused approach.

First, Christianity is much more practical than a post-Enlightenment culture tends to present. Jesus did not come to bring a theory about God but salvation. While the salvation he brought involved theological teachings—some of which challenged traditional ones—the Gospels give as much attention or more to practice: conversion, healing, charity, self-sacrifice, trust in God, and so on. Faith as presented in the Gospels is both content (or, as theologians would say, *fides quae*) and attitude and relationship (*fides qua*). In other words, the salutary relationship with God, and I add, with our fellow human beings, creation, and ourselves, is as important as salutary convictions about God. Here, the words of Pope Benedict in his first encyclical, *Deus Caritas Est*, are worth quoting: "Being Christian is not the result of an ethical choice or a lofty idea, but the encounter

## Witnesses of Synodality

with an event, a person, which gives life a new horizon and a decisive direction." Scripture underlines the practical implications of those relationships: faith needs to be shown by deeds.

Second, the importance of practice relates not only to individuals but also to the church as a body, group, or organization. Indeed, recent scholarship has underlined the notion of "style" as an important aspect of the Second Vatican Council's renewal. Theologians like John O'Malley, Gilles Routhier, and Christophe Theobald have argued that the unicity of the Council goes beyond its words and lies in both what the Council states and how it states it. It wanted to appreciate the world and to engage in conversation rather than to take distance, condemn, and instruct. An intellectual approach is thus complemented by a relational one that promotes the capacity *to listen, to engage in dialogue,* and *to learn.* Synodality too is such a "style." In recent books on synodality, Rafael Luciani speaks of "a new way of proceeding," and Serena Noceti subtitled her book *A Synodal Way of Proceeding.* All this suggests that, for synodality, practice is as important as theory.

## A Common Responsibility

Finally, this book believes that synodality depends on all of us. Alphonse Borras likes to speak about "informal synodality" to underline that synodality is much more than the formalized 2021–24 synodal process. Formal synodality follows canonical rules and involves the pope and bishops. Informal synodality is the everyday practice of journeying together in each of our communities. Theologically, informal synodality is a way of taking seriously that we are all agents or, as Pope Francis states, "protagonists."

That latter conviction is crucial for synodality: the church is primarily the entire people of God, all the baptized, or even all peoples of good will. Synodality challenges overly hierarchical notions of the church that imagine the church as a pyramid. Obviously, the church needs leadership, just as any organization does, and as Christians, we believe that God supports our leaders in their mission. Yet synodality puts baptism first. Before it is useful to speak about the difference between clergy and laity, we should stress that, as baptized, we have all been clothed with Christ and that the Spirit dwells in each and every one of us.

Those theoretical considerations—that need further translation into attitudes, into rules and regulations, and into theology—imply that we should not wait for the bishops to start our synodal conversion. Instead, we should do what is in our reach. It includes developing our own spiritual familiarity with God, so that we can hear what the Spirit is saying to the church. It includes developing listening skills to enter into a constructive and respectful dialogue with our brothers and sisters in church and with those with whom we collaborate. It includes reaching out to the poor so that we may grow in familiarity with Christ's lifestyle and hear the Spirit speaking to us through their laments. And so on.

## Conclusion

I am conscious that this book does not offer a complete set of tools. Conspicuously absent in this book is the wisdom from other Christian churches and from the secular realm. I look forward to reading other books that complement this one. Synodality supposes that everybody contributes something.

Finally, I would like to thank a few people. Thank you to all those we are committed to synodal ways of operating: the General Secretariat of the Synod and its behind-the-scenes collaborators; individuals, groups, religious families, congregations, and orders that attempt to live the ideals of inclusion and participation; the theologians of what I sometimes call "the synodal

## Witnesses of Synodality

family"; and especially those pioneers whose courage is put to the test. I thank the authors for their willingness to put to paper these testimonies. Thanks go to Wilmer Smeenk for multiple consultations. And finally, I have greatly appreciated the wonderful collaboration with Paul McMahon from Paulist Press.

May the Spirit be alive and active in those who pick up this book and in all who work for a more synodal church. Amen.

# 1
# Synodal Wisdom from the Rule of Benedict

*Rebekka Willekes, OCSO*

*Let them prefer nothing whatsoever to Christ
who may bring us all together to life everlasting!* (RB 72.11)[1]

In 2002, I entered Klaarland Priory, a Trappistine monastery in Belgium. At that time, the idea of journeying together with others meant a lot to me. I hoped that the practical support of a community would help me in fulfilling my desire to live for God. Indeed, the fixed timetable and the daily routine of common prayer proved helpful in staying focused on seeking God, living before his face, and responding to his invitation. It was like going on a long hike—not alone but with a companion. At moments of fatigue or low energy, a travel companion would help boost the spirits. We would sing and keep the beat together,

---

1. The quotations from the Rule are taken from *The Rule of St. Benedict in English*, ed. Timothy Fry (Collegeville, MN: Liturgical Press, 1982), and Terence Kardong, *Benedict's Rule: A Translation and Commentary* (Collegeville, MN: Liturgical Press, 1996), with minor adaptations in light of the original Latin.

share our amazement at the surroundings, crack a joke, and so on. Being travel companions is a mutual affair of giving and receiving encouragement.

Over the years, I became more familiar with monastic life. I learned that the Rule of Saint Benedict involves much more than the mutual support and encouragement that I had looked for at the beginning of my monastic journey. Both life and study helped me discover that journeying together is a much more complex—and rich—affair, and that various practices support its realization.

This chapter presents some of those practices that hopefully shed light on the synodal journey that the Catholic Church is currently undertaking. Admittedly, the word "synodality" does not appear in the Rule of Saint Benedict, yet what it represents is at the very heart of Benedictine life: being underway together. Much like a Benedictine community, the church needs to find ways to do just that.

I will first specify two advantages of journeying together. After that, I focus on the Benedictine manner of decision-making that involves ample communal listening before the abbot has the final say. Or should we say, before the Holy Spirit has the final say?

## Journeying Together

*Behold, in His loving kindness the Lord shows us the way of life.*
*Having our loins girded, therefore, with faith and the*
  *performance of good works,*
*let us walk in His paths by the guidance of the Gospel,*
*that we may deserve to see Him who has called us to His*
  *kingdom. (RB Prol 20–21)*

## Synodal Wisdom from the Rule of Benedict

Movement is a major theme in the Rule. The Latin word *via* (way) is featured seventeen times. Saint Benedict often speaks of "going" and, more frequently, of "running" and "hurrying." Even if a monk professes stability and remains in the monastery, he is nevertheless constantly underway: on the way to true life, on the way to truly dwelling in God's presence, and on the way to salvation. "For as we advance in the religious life and in faith, our hearts expand and we run the way of God's commandments with unspeakable sweetness of love" (RB Prol 49).

Thus, like all Christians, monks are people of the way. The final goal has not yet been reached. Every so often, we get lost. Occasionally, we stand still, utterly failing to make progress. It is at these moments that we need traveling companions who encourage or correct us.

Here a great advantage of community life becomes apparent. Brothers and sisters can take you up with them into a rhythm that one desires but does not always have the strength for. When the bell rings, all drop their work to go to church for the singing of psalms, or to the scriptorium for feeding the soul through *lectio divina*. While it is obvious that each Christian and every human person, both inside the monastery and outside, has one's own path, we also need to journey together. More than we care to admit in this age of individualism, we need travel companions who are heading toward the same goal, and who provide encouragement and critical questions, not to mention help when someone has fallen or cannot continue. Benedict makes this mutual support very concrete. "When they rise for the Work of God [i.e., singing the office], let them gently encourage one another, that the drowsy may have no excuse" (RB 22.8).[2]

---

[2]. On a personal note: I must say that, when the alarm clock rings early in the morning for our first prayer service, it helps that others are expecting me in church.

## Witnesses of Synodality

# The Community as the Way, the Truth, and the Life

*They should most patiently endure one another's infirmities, whether of body or of character.*
*No one should seek what he considers useful for himself, but rather what benefits others.* (RB 72.5.7)

Having experienced these benefits of fellow sisters for several years, I discovered that community life entails much more than encouragement and correction. In journeying together, the aspect of "together" is as helpful as the road itself. Christ is not just the end point of the road, but he is found in the very living together as the body of Christ. "No man is an island entire of itself."[3] No one can do everything, and nobody needs to be able to do everything, for when one cannot do something, one's neighbor may help. Gifts and talents are not supposed to be kept for oneself but are for the community. In a homily for the feast of Saint Benedict, Aelred of Rievaulx, a twelfth-century Cistercian abbot, formulated:

> No one therefore should boast on his own about any grace given by God as if it were exclusively his own. No one should envy his brother because of some grace, as if it were exclusively his. Whatever he has, he should consider the property of all his brothers, and whatever his brother has, he should never doubt is also his. Almighty God can immediately bring to perfection anyone he pleases and bestow all the virtues on any one person. But in his caring way [of] dealing with us he causes each person to need the other and

---

3. John Donne, *Devotions upon Emergent Occasions*, ed. Anthony Raspa (Montreal: McGill-Queen's University Press, 1975), 87.

## Synodal Wisdom from the Rule of Benedict

to have in the other what one does not possess in oneself. Thus humility is preserved, charity increased and unity recognized. Therefore each belongs to all and all belong to each. Thus each has the benefit of the virtues while preserving humility by the consciousness of individual weakness.[4]

Thus, God intentionally wants us not to be perfect and self-sufficient. Relationships of mutual dependence are essential. When Jesus sent out his disciples, he did so in pairs (cf. Luke 10:1-4). He did not allow them to take anything with them—no purse, no travel bag, no footwear—except for a brother.

Maybe the point here is that they might help one another. Perhaps Jesus wanted them not only to *talk* about the kingdom of God that had come near in Christ but also to live and to proclaim its reality from their own experience. Their brotherly love, friendship, and mutual attention—their fraternal communion in Christ—was what they lived and invited others to. Their *missio* was *communio*, both as a purpose and as a method.

That is, of course, the ideal. In a monastic community, no different from any other context, fraternal love is hard work. Saint Benedict is aware of this and specifies in considerable detail how brothers—or, in our case, sisters—should treat one another. I am impressed by the balance he finds between accepting a brother's imperfection, on the one hand, and urging him to do as much as he can, on the other. Benedict is both lenient and demanding and expects as much of the abbot. He must arrange everything with discernment and measure, in such a way that something is left for the strong to desire while the weak are not deterred (RB 64.19). In other words, in a monastic community one should appreciate everyone's abilities and tolerate with great patience

---

4. Aelred of Rievaulx. *The Liturgical Sermons: Advent–All Saints*, Cistercian Father Series 58 (Collegeville, MN: Liturgical Press, 2008), Sermon Eight, 147–54, at 150.

one another's physical as well as moral weaknesses, while also helping one another to grow.

## Listening to One Another to Understand the Spirit

*Do everything with counsel.* (RB 3.13)

    *Communio* is thus both the end goal and the journey. This is also reflected in the way decisions are taken. While the Rule grants the abbot a large say, he cannot decide by himself as he likes. An initial limitation is the Rule itself. The abbot must abide by the Rule and cannot change it at will. Second, Benedict warns that the abbot will be accountable to the Lord. "The Abbot himself should do all things in the fear of God and in observance of the Rule, knowing that beyond a doubt he will have to render an account of all his decisions to God, the most just Judge" (RB 3.11). And third, according to the Rule, the abbot should seek counsel from the brethren. Evidently, Benedict's method is not a democratic process where most votes count but rather a process of discernment. Just like a synodal process, the abbot decides in the end; and just like a synodal process, listening and seeking together are fundamental. As the Rule notes:

> Whenever there is something important to deal with
>    in the monastery,
> let the abbot call together the whole community
> and state the matter at stake.
> Then, having heard the brethren's advice,
> let him turn the matter over in his own mind
> and do what he shall judge best.
> The reason why we have said that all should be
>    called for deliberation

is that the Lord often reveals what is best to the
younger person.

Let the brethren give their advice in all humility and
submission,
and not presume stubbornly to defend their
opinions;
but let the decision rather depend on the abbot's
judgment,
and all submit to whatever he shall decide for their
welfare. (RB 3.1–5)

The first step is for the abbot to gather the entire community. It is the abbot's task to ensure that the necessary information is given so that everyone knows what the deliberation is about. Informing the brothers carefully indicates that their input is taken seriously. Their knowledge must be such that it allows them to look at the matter from all sides and give real advice.

Let me stress that *all* are called together. In practice, it sometimes seems easier to consult with a few confidants, or even to decide by oneself. It goes faster and causes less turmoil in the community. But I keep discovering how useful it is to consult with the entire community. Arguments come up that I had not thought of, and the conversation clarifies the true weight of various considerations. Thus, the process is much more than just asking everyone's opinion, after which the superior makes up her mind and takes a decision. For that, a survey would be sufficient. Being together and listening to everyone's input makes us all grow closer to one another and reach the best decision. In practice, then, it is usual that, after one or more conversations, the direction we should go becomes clear to the prioress and the sisters, even though that conviction may not be unanimous.

No one is excluded from the meeting, and the youngest ones should be listened to with particular attention, for "the

# Witnesses of Synodality

Lord often reveals to the younger person what is best." Thus, Benedict values two forms of wisdom. First, there is the wisdom of the experienced elders. In the monastic life, one's place in the line of monks or sisters is determined by the number of years spent in the monastery. "Thus, for example, he who came to the monastery at the second hour of the day should know that he is junior to one who came at the first hour of the day, no matter what his age or status" (RB 63.8). What matters is not social position or age but monastic experience, in other words, how long one has been formed by the Rule and the community.

Second, however, there is room for the ideas of the younger members. "We have always done it this way" does not mean that it should always *stay* this way. It may well be through a young person that the Lord reveals what is best, as such a person is less bound to the established customs. Benedict is open to new perspectives. Interestingly, the "Preparatory Document" for the Synod on Synodality quotes this section precisely from the Rule.[5] Benedict's openness is such that even a remark by a monk from outside, one who stays as a guest in the monastery, will make him wonder if the Lord has sent him precisely to that end (RB 61.4).

This "counsel" or meeting consists of listening and speaking. The listening part presupposes great openness in the form of a desire to hear what the other person has to say. For example, while another person is speaking, I might be musing about what I am going to say when it is my turn to speak. The type of meeting Benedict intends, however, is not so much about what I may want to say, but rather what I may hear. Or rather, what the Lord wants me to hear and, thereby, to reveal to me. Therefore, it is crucial that everybody is listened to and that, even when *I* speak, I listen carefully to what I am saying.

---

5. Secretariat to the Synod, "Preparatory Document," no. 14 (September 7, 2021). It refers to Saint Benedict's instruction to listen to all, including the youngest, to support the idea that the bishops should consult widely.

## Synodal Wisdom from the Rule of Benedict

When speaking, therefore, Benedict stipulates that the brothers or sisters "give their advice in all humility and submission." This may seem far removed from the usual twenty-first-century style of conversation. The aim is that one should speak with modesty and with a readiness to listen. Interestingly, a more literal translation of the phrase "in all humility and submission" (*cum omni humilitatis subiectione*, RB 3.4, also RB 6.7) suggests that we should not focus on the abbot. The point here is not to "humbly" say what you think the abbot wants to hear. Rather, the focus is on the matter at hand; the goal of my speaking should be to allow God's light to enlighten the topic. Thus, I am not present in the meeting to defend my opinion but rather to hope that my speaking may help the community reach clarity.

In fact, Benedict asks for a *double* humility.[6] The first humility is simply to share what you think. Not saying anything may be a form of pride: Do I remain silent to avoid the impression that what I have to say is not very intelligent? For Benedict, all contributions play a role in the process and help to find the right path, including views that will not be followed in the end or imperfect views. The second humility is the readiness to give up one's view without being stubborn. Everyone's input is a service to the community, but it is equally important to keep moving: to listen to how the conversation develops and how a shared conviction grows.

Finally, according to Benedict, "let the decision rather depend on the abbot's judgment." It is ultimately the abbess's responsibility to taking a decision. She cannot hide behind the majority. But at the same time, the decision has been maturing in the communal process outlined above. The abbess listens and ponders what she hears. The dialogue in the community is not a superficial matter but feeds the abbess's personal meditation. Just as Mary reflected in her heart upon the words of the shepherds, so

---

6. Humility is dealt with extensively in chapter 7, "On Humility," of the Rule.

does the abbess contemplate the words of her sisters, and thus, in the silence of her prayer, the decision takes shape.

In my experience, this "reflecting in her heart" happens for all the sisters, not just the abbess. It usually takes (some) time to let go of one's own ideas and to see the wisdom of another perspective. If all goes well, the whole community grows toward a decision.

There is always the risk that I take my own opinion for the will of God all along. In that case, I am just trying to convince the other sisters without leaving space for the Lord to say something different. Another danger is omitting the phase of prayerful consideration and simply following the voice of the majority. That is easy, for counting votes is quickly done and generally accepted in democratic times, but it is not listening to the Spirit.

## Obedience

When a decision has been taken or a course established, Benedict supposes that all obey the abbot in what he has judged best. Confident that we have listened to one another and to the Lord, the community supports the outcome and moves forward together. This raises two questions. First, as a prioress, am I sure that I have listened carefully and that what I have decided is the will of God? Second, as a brother or sister, if I am convinced that the decision is not right, should I still accept it?

Regarding the second question, it is always possible to talk. Benedict included a chapter in the Rule on what a brother should do when ordered to perform an impossible task (RB 68). The brother should both question his own difficulties with the abbot's words, without assuming that he is right, and question the abbot. The abbot may be wrong also. Obedience is not *blind* obedience. Objections can be articulated within the monastery or, if necessary, outside of it. Monasteries are part of a larger context, first the order, then also the church. Listening goes beyond one's own community.

The first question is especially interesting. Even if I listen to the best of my ability, in dialogue with all the sisters and in the silence of prayer, it may happen that I decide or that we choose a path together that later turns out not to be the right one. With some envy I read that the apostles and elders of Jerusalem introduce their decisions with "it has seemed good to the Holy Spirit and to us…" (Acts 15:28). Can one be so firmly convinced that we want the same thing as the Spirit?

I can only say that, when there is a sense of peace, communion, and joy, these are strong indications that a decision does come from the Spirit. With that, our human limitations have not disappeared. There may be things we did not foresee, so that in hindsight the decision was not the right one. It may be that, as a community, we are not yet ready for what, in fact, is the better decision; in that case, our pettiness stands in the way. Or we simply err and take the wrong decision. However, I believe that the Spirit also works through our wrong decisions. Our imperfections do not stop God. If we keep listening to one another, striving to discern together the way the Lord is pointing, He can also lead us to the *communio* with Him that is both our final goal and our journey with a diversion.

## Conclusion

So far, I have spoken from the monastic setting. What wisdom might Saint Benedict have to share for a parish community, a diocese, or other groups of people?

First, synodality means that we are journeying together, as companions on the road. The person who thinks that he or she has already arrived, or that it is easier to reach the destination alone, might well be overestimating him- or herself. The ancient

## Witnesses of Synodality

Rule of Saint Benedict helps to point out the blind spots of our age, which places great emphasis on independence and self-development. We need one another's help and support.

Second, a community is more than just a practical support along the way. The gospel is an invitation to friendship with God and with one another in Christ. Everyone belongs to that community, there is no need to be perfect. Even at his betrayal, Jesus addressed Judas as "friend." Thus, a synodal community also means tolerating one another in our imperfections.

Third, the first word of the Rule is "Listen!" That may well be more interesting than proclaiming one's own opinion all the time, and it is certainly crucial for synodality. "To honor all people" (RB 4.8) by listening attentively to their input keeps us open to the creativity of the Spirit.

Finally, obedience is a realistic, nonperfectionist attitude that relativizes one's own beliefs. The community may reach a different decision from what I thought best. Even if the decision is wrong or imperfect, if we keep listening to one another, the Spirit will find a way to lead us back. I personally find it exciting and hopeful that it is precisely by failing in my project and accepting a different path that something new becomes possible. Just like when we are on a hike and the others are convinced that we should turn left while I am sure the route goes right. We may be straying from the official route, but who knows what unexpected, beautiful places we will now pass by?

## Bibliography

Aelred of Rievaulx. *The Liturgical Sermons: Advent–All Saints*. Cistercian Father Series 58. Collegeville, MN: Liturgical Press, 2008.

Böckmann, Aquinata. *Around the Monastic Table*. Collegeville, MN: Liturgical Press, 2009.

## Synodal Wisdom from the Rule of Benedict

Fry, Timothy, ed. *The Rule of St. Benedict in English*. Collegeville, MN: Liturgical Press, 1982.

Kardong, Terence. *Benedict's Rule: A Translation and Commentary*. Collegeville, MN: Liturgical Press, 1996.

Lepori, Mauro Giuseppe, OCist. "Synodality of Communion: Letter of the Abbot General for Pentecost 2022." https://www.ocist.org/ocist/images/pdf/ENPentecost2022.pdf.

Secretariat to the Synod. "Preparatory Document." September 7, 2021.

Vesco, Jean-Paul. *L'Amitié*. Montrouge: Bayard, 2017.

Williams, Rowan. *The Way of St Benedict*. London: Bloomsbury, 2020.

# 2

# Dominican Gifts for a Synodal Church

*Stefan Mangnus, OP*

Whenever Dominicans get asked what we love most about our religious order, one of the first things often mentioned is "our constitutions." To many, this might be a surprising answer. It sounds sobering, matter of fact, and perhaps even uninspiring to refer to constitutions as one of the most outstanding qualities of an order. Yet, it is a shared experience of many Dominicans that the constitutions of our order do more than create organizational conditions. It is both through the content of the constitutions and how they function within the Order of Preachers that much of the Dominican charism becomes visible.

This chapter presents some of the gifts that the Order of Preachers can offer to a synodal church. Most of these gifts are directly related to our constitutions and the "style" of living religious life that characterizes our order. The constitutions used in this chapter are those of the Dominican brothers. I hope that the Dominican contemplative nuns, Dominican sisters, and lay Dominicans will recognize many of the underlying ideas from their regulations and how they are practiced.

Dominican Gifts for a Synodal Church

# Maturity and Flexibility

In 1220, the first general chapter of the Order of the Preachers was held in Bologna. The foundations for the order's constitutions were laid during this first chapter and the second one that was held a year later. From the outset, these constitutions have made room for development. Any general chapter may propose amendments to the texts of the constitutions, which then get discussed during the next general chapter, and definitively approved at a third. Because general chapters are held at least every three years, a change in the constitutions can be made in six years. Dominican law was never crystallized into a rigid text but has remained flexible through the centuries. It continues to evolve to meet the needs of changing times and circumstances.

While until then, disobedience to the rule was often regarded as sin in religious orders, Saint Dominic himself emphasized that our constitutions do not oblige under sin. It is even said that he threatened that if the brothers would become overly scrupulous and too obsessed with following the constitutions, he would come with a knife and cut up the copies! Legendary or not, the story illustrates a way of dealing with our order's constitutions: the constitutions serve the mission of the order, and the brothers are to use them in a mature way.

The maturity expected of a brother is stressed in other ways as well. From the beginning of his novitiate, a brother is expected to take responsibility for his formation, and time and again in the constitutions the responsibility and personal gifts of the brothers are approached positively and encouraged: a brother is called to express his maturity in the way he lives the vows, in prayer, in his apostolate, in the chapters in which he participates, and in the elections in which he has the right to vote.

What matters is that the constitutions free the brothers for the mission of the order: the proclamation of the gospel. This

## Witnesses of Synodality

focus on the mission can also be seen in the rule of dispensation that is already mentioned as a principle in the oldest constitutions and formulated remarkably broadly. For the sake of preaching, but also for reasons of study or for reasons that touch on the salvation of people, dispensation is possible for most of our rules. In the practice of the order, this functions with a certain self-evidence: dispensation may be assumed for many matters that directly affect the mission of the order, and in many other situations, a brother may receive dispensation from a superior. It shows a religious culture in which mature people deal with rules and hierarchical relationships in a shared responsibility.

The Dominican practice of regularly reviewing its constitutions has something to offer a church that wants to grow in synodality. A synodal church is, by nature, a church in development. The ongoing and regulated process of reviewing and confirming our constitutions expresses the recognition that the conditions for the order's preaching mission are constantly changing. The mission to preach at the heart of the Dominican charism is, of course, the same mission to proclaim the gospel that is the task of the whole church. Consequently, it would be wise for a church that is rediscovering its synodality to look for ways to review laws and rules regularly that apply in the church (also but not exclusively in synodal processes themselves) and, where necessary, to adapt and reconfirm them because of the church's mission in ever-changing times and cultures.

The Dominican mature approach to the constitutions, with the emphasis on every brother's responsibility and in the principle of the dispensation, is also helpful for a synodal church. The church becomes synodal only insofar as it considers all its baptized members as adults. This has two sides. Every baptized person, on the one hand, may be held accountable for their contribution to the church's mission. After all, every Christian

## Dominican Gifts for a Synodal Church

believer shares in Christ's royal, priestly, and prophetic office through baptism (see *Lumen Gentium* 10–13). This participation becomes concrete when all the baptized use their talents for the common good. On the other hand, regarding all the baptized as adults requires taking them seriously as mature believers. When people are infantilized, their voices are not heard, or justified hierarchical distinctions degenerate into power structures in which the majority of the people of God are, de facto, deprived of all authority, the church loses its synodal character, and its credibility is compromised.

## Dominican Democracy

From the beginning, the Dominican order has been organized democratically. Whether it is the house chapter for a house or a priory, the provincial chapter for a province, or the general chapter for an entire order, the highest authority at all levels in the order lies with the assembly of brothers who consult together and make decisions for all matters entrusted to their responsibility. The order has superiors at various levels who hold ecclesiastical jurisdiction and are elected for a fixed term. At each level, however, the supreme authority rests with the chapter, of which the members are elected.

In practice, this means that we often vote in elections and on matters under discussion. Voting processes usually take place in two stages. The first stage is a conversation in which ideas are presented, opinions are shared, and consensus is sought. This pursuit of unity forms the heart of the democratic process in our order. The main question is, How do we become of one soul and one spirit?

Conversation leads to a vote—the second stage. The results of the vote sometimes show that a chapter has succeeded in finding unity. When that unanimity has not been

## Witnesses of Synodality

found, the (sometimes qualified) majority of votes counts as the decision of the entire chapter, including those who voted in opposition.

How can Dominican democracy be helpful for the church? Voting happens in many places in the church: popes are elected, and votes are taken at councils and synods, just as in episcopal conferences. Yet people sometimes prefer to avoid the word "democracy," either because the church is not a democracy or because there is a concern for division and polarization. This concern for division and polarization is valid, and the church is not a democracy, if only because the church does not derive its existence from itself but receives it from God. However, this does not exclude appropriate democratic forms of decision-making and voting. Saint Dominic organized the Dominican order democratically, not because he thought the majority is always right but because he believed the Holy Spirit was poured out on each of the brothers; everyone has something to say. Therefore, in the Dominican order, it is part of the dignity of a brother that he has the right to vote.

Two things are important here. The first is *representation*. Dominican democracy is a representative democracy: in elections, the brothers are chosen who will participate in a provincial chapter and have the right to vote, and likewise, each province sends a representative delegation to a general chapter. A more synodal church would do well to reflect on proper representation. How is a member elected or appointed to an administrative body? Once elected or appointed, who does a representative represent? Only herself? A group? Does a young person speak on behalf of young people? A religious on behalf of the religious? A woman on behalf of women? There are questions like these at all levels in the church, and for the proper functioning of democratic forms of decision-making, it is necessary to find appropriate forms of representation.

Second, the timing of the voting is crucial, as Timothy Radcliffe has remarked.[1] If a vote is taken too soon, the debate may not have had the chance to develop sufficiently, or the brothers may not have had enough time to speak. It is essential to ask why some people do not speak. Is it a silence of misunderstanding or incomprehension? Are people silent out of fear, anger, or confusion? It must be made easy for people to speak, especially those who are silent, and if people have not had a chance to express doubts or reservations, the moment to vote has not yet arrived. If people have not had an opportunity to speak openly, they will not accept the outcome of the vote as a shared decision. Voting too late, however, can also be problematic: indications that a group has taken too long to vote include people becoming bored and the conversation getting stuck.

## Patience

Democracy is a process that requires care and attention. In his book on reforms in the church, Yves Congar describes four conditions for authentic ecclesial reforms: first, good reforms must give priority to love and pastoral care rather than to maintaining a system; second, it is necessary to remain in communion with the whole church because the whole truth can only be understood with the whole church; third, it is necessary to have patience with delays; and fourth, genuine reforms come about through a return to the sources.[2] Each of these four conditions is meaningful for a synodal church, but I note the third in particular: the importance of patience and the tolerance of delays.

---

1. Timothy Radcliffe, "The Spirituality of Dominican Government," lecture given in Oxford, February 2014, see https://www.youtube.com/watch?v=nM5mmUFCDFM.

2. Yves Congar, *True and False Reform in the Church*, trans. Paul Philibert (Collegeville, MN: Liturgical Press, 2011; orig. French, 2nd ed.: Paris: Cerf, 1968), 199–307.

# Witnesses of Synodality

Patience is not much encouraged in our Western societies, and many people find it challenging to deal with the uncertainty that arises when a case is undecided. Democratic processes are inherently slow and seldom efficient. Patience is even more difficult when trust in ecclesial structures is low; it is not easy to trust a process when people have recent experiences in which processes were undermined by delaying tactics or other abuses of power.

Trust is slowly won and quickly lost. Where trust has been lost, that loss must be recognized, and serious efforts must be made to do justice to those who have lost faith in the church. At all times, synodal processes must be transparent and inclusive. Even when a basic trust in the synodal process is present, there is always the danger of a lack of patience. In the Dominican order, it is common to take time to search for consensus. In other words, have an extra meeting to think things over and try to reach a consensus rather than have a situation in which a group forces through controversial decisions. Impatience can be very destructive.

The patience required in this form of democracy is not just a resigned acceptance of reality (the church just moves slowly) but a flexibility of mind that can be understood as a conscious choice to reject perfectionism. Congar, who knew his own impatience—"I can't even wait for a bus!" he once exclaimed—noticed that patience implies not falling for the temptation of an "all or nothing" or "now or never" mentality. Developments in the church should be allowed to proceed step-by-step and take time. To have that patience, to encourage one another in it, without falling into indecisiveness but for the sake of a process in which great value is attached to unity, is of great importance for a synodal church.

Conducting a good process is an art. When I moved to Rotterdam with a group of brothers to form a new community a few years ago, our provincial council decided that we would receive external supervision in forming the new community.

That worked very well. We, seven brothers in total, had never lived together in a house before, so in this new community, we had to discover how to work together, how to make decisions together, what each of us needed to feel at home in this new house, and what would be appropriate and helpful for us to shape our religious community life. The outside supervisor made it possible for us to speak with one another freely and on an equal footing and helped us learn how to listen to what was hidden beneath the words of each brother. In synodal processes, the manner of conducting the proceedings is vital. In recent decades, a great deal of expertise has emerged in this area: there are experts on organizational development, process facilitation, and conflict resolution, people who know what is involved in processes of change and decision-making issues. Among these experts are many who know the Catholic Church from the inside or are open to learning its ways. That expertise could be used much more than is often customary in the church: it will help the church to have better, more synodal processes.

## Obedience as Learning

Dominicans take only one vow: the vow of obedience. Because it is the only vow we take, it is particularly important to us. In our society, obedience often gets a bad reputation: it is misunderstood as a violation of a person's maturity, freedom, or integrity. The hesitation toward obedience, understood as blindly surrendering to someone else's will, makes sense. There is a long history of abuse of this kind of obedience, both in the church and in society.

Obedience can be understood differently. It has often been noted that "obedience" comes from the Latin *ob-audire*; obedience begins with listening. It is that to which the people of Israel

## Witnesses of Synodality

have been called time and again through the ages: "Hear, O Israel, the Lord is our God, the Lord alone" (Deut 6:4). To obey is to listen with the desire to learn from the other.

Thomas Aquinas went one step further. For him, to command (*imperare*) is primarily something of the mind; the will is involved, but it is not primary. To command is the act of someone who understands what must be done. Obedience is responding to this. Obedience brings people together to be of one mind. The job of a superior is not to make their will prevail but to lead the educational process by which the good for a community becomes clear to everyone, the superior himself included. As Herbert McCabe famously wrote, "The notion of blind obedience makes no more sense in our tradition than would blind learning."[3]

This understanding of obedience is valuable for a church that wants to become more synodal. Synodality is not just about governance, about who gets to have a say in decision-making processes in the church. Synodality puts the learning process at the heart of governance. This has significant consequences for how we talk about this process. Words like "commandment" or, if someone does not agree with what is being said, "dissent" are inappropriate to describe what is happening. How should one speak when people do not follow what is presented in the synodal process? "Disagreement" seems a better term. After all, part of a learning process is that people ask questions and speak up if they do not understand something or disagree with what is being said. One cannot go through a learning process based on authority alone. What would happen if something were "taught" based on authority alone? Thomas Aquinas answered that question when he wrote, "If a teacher determines a question with bare authorities, the hearer will indeed be assured that something is so, but he will acquire no science or understanding

---

3. Herbert McCabe, *God Matters* (London: Continuum, 1987), 229.

and will go away with an empty head."⁴ The learning process of synodality cannot be conducted based on authority alone but must be conducted based on content and arguments, on listening carefully to understand what concerns and personal histories resonate when someone raises an objection.

This does not mean, of course, that there is no place for governance in the church: the church has all too often been damaged when governance was not carried out with due diligence. But commands do not teach. Growing into a more synodal church means rediscovering that the church's teaching is a doctrine that seeks to educate, not just command. Synodal decision-making is a form of learning together.⁵

How do we deal with situations where people have been hurt or become angry? During debates, tempers can run high, and things that are dear and sacred to one person can get trampled on by another. The general recommendation here is not to force a solution but to initiate a process. Timothy Radcliffe once related how a conflict arose during a general chapter about how the gospel should be preached. Some brothers, especially from Asia, argued for dialogue. Some other brothers, particularly those from Eastern Europe who had lived under communism, argued for a strong proclamation of the truth that does not shun controversy. The profound disagreement blocked the chapter for a long time. It was impossible to resolve the question during the chapter, so a commission was set up with representatives from the various groups. For several years, that group worked to understand how each brother's experiences colored his view of preaching.⁶ What should we do when a conversation gets stuck? Do not force a solution, but look for ways to initiate a process.

---

4. Thomas Aquinas, *Questiones de Quodlibet*, IV, q. 9, a. 3.

5. For more on the relation between governance and teaching, see Nicholas Lash, "Oracles, Dissent, and Conversation: Reflections on Catholic Teaching," in *The Contested Legacy of Vatican II: Lessons and Prospects*, ed. L. Boeve, M. Lamberigts, and T. Merrigan (Leuven: Peeters, 2015), 125–52.

6. Radcliffe, "The Spirituality of Dominican Government."

## Witnesses of Synodality

After all, the alternative is to fall apart. That has never been an option for our order, and it cannot be an option for a church that sees itself as synodal.

# The Value of Debate

It is one of the Dominicans' most beloved origin stories: On a journey through the Albigensian region of southern France, Dominic meets an innkeeper who is a Cathar. Dominic and the innkeeper talk all night long, and when the sun rises, they are both profoundly changed; the innkeeper returns to the Catholic Church, and Dominic has found his calling. An Irish Dominican is said to have remarked that we do not know what the innkeeper and Dominic discussed through the night, but we do know that Dominic cannot just have repeated all night long, "You are wrong, you are wrong, you are wrong." It must have been a real conversation in which each man was moved by what the other had to say.

The fact that this story is so popular in Dominican circles shows a religious culture with a love for debate. It is essential to keep the aim of the debate in mind: the purpose of a debate is not to defeat the other but to come closer to a shared truth. This can be seen in a stylized way in Thomas Aquinas's *Summa Theologiae*. In that work, which consists entirely of debates, Thomas always gives arguments for two opposing positions in a discussion and then chooses a position himself. However, he does not stop there. After Thomas has chosen his position, he revisits the original arguments and indicates what truth can be found there. The latter is essential. Even if the positions taken seem squarely opposed to each other, Thomas actively searches for whatever truth can be found in each position. For Thomas, this is not merely a matter of courtesy but a choice of faith. He often quotes a phrase from Pseudo-Ambrose: "Every truth, spoken by whoever comes from the Holy Spirit."

## Dominican Gifts for a Synodal Church

The love for debate that characterizes the Dominican tradition is pertinent to synodality. It is not self-evident in our culture: no political debate passes without the media reporting who has "won" the debate. Speaking freely in church, without fear of reprisal, in the vulnerability that the other person might convince me and with the desire to discover the truth in what the other person has to say, is not self-evident. If the starting point is the joint search for truth and for what the Holy Spirit is trying to say through our words and our listening, the debate brings joy and can happily go on all night.

## Conclusion

I have presented a few gifts that the Dominican order has to offer to a church that is becoming more synodal: the importance of a mature way of dealing with rules and of regularly reconsidering them, the discovery of democratic forms of decision-making that are proper to the church, and attention to representation and the timing of voting. I have suggested that it is important not to rush processes and not to be afraid to ask for help from knowledgeable outsiders. These practices have benefitted the Dominican order, some of them for many centuries. They can also benefit a synodal church.

## Bibliography

The Book of Constitutions and Ordinations of the Brothers of the Order of Preachers. www.op.org/documents/.
Aquinas, Thomas. *Summa Theologiae*. Translated by Thomas Gilby et. al. London: Eyre and Spottiswoode, 1964-73 ("Blackfriars edition").

## Witnesses of Synodality

———. *Thomas Aquinas's Quodlibetal Questions*. Translated and introduced by Turner Nevitt and Brian Davies. Oxford: Oxford University Press, 2019.

Congar, Yves. *True and False Reform in the Church*. Translated by Paul Philibert. Collegeville MN: Liturgical Press, 2011. Original French 2nd ed.: Paris: Editions du Cerf, 1968.

Lash, Nicholas. "Oracles, Dissent, and Conversation: Reflections on Catholic Teaching." In *The Contested Legacy of Vatican II: Lessons and Prospects*, edited by L. Boeve, M. Lamberigts, and T. Merrigan, 125–52. Leuven: Peeters, 2015.

McCabe, Herbert. *God Matters*. London: Continuum, 1987.

Radcliffe, Timothy. "Freedom and Responsibility: Toward a Spirituality of Government." In *Sing a New Song: The Christian Vocation*, 82–120. Dublin: Dominican Publications, 1999.

———. "The Spirituality of Dominican Government." Lecture given in Oxford, February 2014. See https://youtu.be/nM5mmUFCDFM.

# 3

# A Franciscan Approach to Synodality

*Noel Muscat, OFM*

The Franciscan family is one of the largest spiritual families in the church. Inspired by Saint Francis of Assisi (1181–1226) and his companion Saint Clare (1194–1253), it includes the Franciscans, the Conventuals, the Capuchins, the Poor Clares, and a rich variety of Franciscan sisters, to mention but the major ones. Their origin dates to the thirteenth century, a period of revival that saw a desire for evangelical simplicity alongside a desire for preaching the gospel. Concrete manifestations of this revival were the so-called mendicant orders, known especially for the Friars Preachers (Dominicans) and the Friars Minor (Franciscans). Clearly, God walks with his people and raises the kind of saints that each time needs!

Supposing that the Franciscan charism is still a gift to the church, this chapter explores how it may enlighten the current synodal journey. For that I draw on both historical details related

### Witnesses of Synodality

to the founding of the Franciscan family and on the contemporary way of living the Franciscan charism.

## *Fratres Minores:* On Leadership and Service

There is some irony in the name that we have been using so far—especially, the Franciscans and the Franciscan family—for Francis promoted a rather different name: *fratres minores*, "minor brothers." The Rule that was approved by Pope Honorius III on November 29, 1223, some eight hundred year ago, opens with the words, "The Rule and Life of the *fratres minores* is this: to observe the holy gospel of our Lord Jesus Christ by living in obedience, without anything of one's own, and in chastity."[1] The point was not just to have a written Rule approved; rather, Saint Francis insisted that this Rule was the expression of their commitment to following the poor and crucified Christ.

The novelty of this form of life becomes apparent in the choice for the term "minor brothers." Already in the so-called *Earlier Rule* (1221), Francis had stipulated that those in leadership should not be called "prior" (literally, "who comes first"), as was usual, but that all should bear the same name: "Let no one be called *prior*, but let everyone in general be called a friar minor. Let one wash the feet of the other."[2] In an early biography, brother Thomas of Celano ascribes this choice to Francis's own inspiration. Celano writes,

> Francis himself originally planted the Order of Friars Minor and on the occasion of its founding gave it this

---

[1]. *Later Rule*, c. 1, in Francis of Assisi, *Early Documents* I, ed. R. J. Armstrong, W. J. Hellmann, and W. Short (New York: New City Press, 1999), 100.

[2]. *Earlier Rule*, c. 6, in Francis of Assisi, *Early Documents* I, 68.

name. For when it was written in the Rule, "Let them be minors...," at the uttering of this statement, at the same moment he said, "I want this fraternity to be called the Order of Friars Minor."[3]

This affects leadership. While leadership roles cannot be avoided, Francis wanted the superiors to be called by the name *minister et servus*, "minister and servant." The highest leader is called "general minister," and provinces have a "provincial minister." As for houses, they are led by a "guardian," literally "somebody who guards." These terms were meant to underline the attitude of humble service inspired by Jesus washing the feet of the brethren that should characterize leadership roles. This notion is based upon the words of Jesus: "The greatest among you must become like the youngest, and the leader like one who serves" (Luke 22:26).

The focus on service is also clear in the functioning of the chapter—the gathering of the brothers (or sisters) to take major decisions—and the approach to mission. Inherited from the monastic tradition, chapters are a common practice in religious life. Francis, however, saw the chapter as a new Pentecost: led by the Spirit, the order would send people on a mission. Indeed, for Francis, "the Holy Spirit is the true General Minister of the Order."[4] Sent out to evangelize Christians and nonbelievers alike and to journey along the roads of this world, the brothers were to give witness to Christ primarily silently, by their way of Christian life, and they were to preach only when they discerned that it was God's will. As Francis notes in chapter 16 of the *Earlier Rule*:

> As for the brothers who go, they can live spiritually among the Saracens and nonbelievers in two ways.

---

3. Thomas of Celano, *The Life of Saint Francis*, 38, in Francis of Assisi, *Early Documents* I, 38.

4. Thomas of Celano, *The Remembrance of the Desire of a Soul*, 193, in Francis of Assisi, *Early Documents* II, 371.

### Witnesses of Synodality

> One way is not to engage in arguments or disputes but to be subject to every human creature for God's sake and to acknowledge that they are Christians. The other way is to announce the Word of God, when they see it pleases the Lord.[5]

The humble and service-oriented Franciscan style of life, leadership, and mission was an innovation in the church and is still relevant, especially for the current synodal journey. Fraternal life in "minority" shows that we can build an ecclesial community, in which we learn how to listen to one another, collaborate, and share our resources. It extends beyond the familiar circle to others, including nonbelievers and even creation, in general, entailing openness to dialogue, even amid tensions. It calls for a courageous option for justice and peace, for the poor of today's world, and for respect toward the environment, without exploitation and domination. Synodal leadership, too, should be that of humble service. An attitude of service is an essential building block for journeying together in a relationship built not upon hierarchy but upon brotherhood—in other words, for synodality.

## A History with Twists and Turns

Beyond the origins of the Franciscan family, inspiration for the current synodal process can also be found in its subsequent history. Admittedly, that history is not always glorious. I often compare the Franciscan order with the whole church. Just as church history in general includes periods of revival and decline, openness and closure, reaching out and self-defense, union and division, so too does the Franciscan history.

---

5. *Regula non bullata*, c. 16, in Francis of Assisi, *Early Documents* I, 74–75. Importantly, this is the earliest example of a chapter dedicated to missionary evangelization in the Rule of a religious order.

## A Franciscan Approach to Synodality

For example, throughout the eight hundred years of its history, deep divisions have risen among the daughters and sons of Saint Francis. This has resulted in a great number of "family members," among which are the three major male branches: Franciscans, Conventuals, and Capuchins, alongside many others. Whenever Franciscans felt that the order had become too institutionalized and too sedentary, they embarked upon new reforms. This is what happened in the early fourteenth century in the reform of the "Spirituals" and Fraticelli, who opted for a greater faithfulness to Francis's original inspiration and insisted on the fact that Christ and the apostles possessed nothing on an individual or communal level. The way of life of the reformed brothers created tension but was providential in reminding the order and the papal curia of the need to listen to the grassroots yearning for a return to Francis's interpretation of the gospel.[6]

One can be rightly scandalized by these divisions. Indeed, journeying together is not easy, as we know from our own experience with family life, collaboration with colleagues, and so on. At the same time, these very divisions in the Franciscan family throughout its history speak of life and depth. The divisions are the result of a sincere quest for encountering Christ and for embracing anew the way of life of the gospel in all its radicality. In other words, they express a genuine desire for listening to what the Spirit was telling the Franciscan family at a given moment. Moreover, can we say, therefore, that the Spirit has been trying to teach the Franciscan family about unity in diversity, despite many mistakes and inner divisions?

On a more positive note, the history of the Franciscan family witnesses to great flexibility and creativity when it comes to discerning the signs of the times and embracing new missions.

---

6. Some of these brothers were regarded as heretics, because they were proposing an ideology of poverty that went against canon law. In fact, they fully belonged to the Franciscan family. One of their sympathizers even became minister general of the order, namely John Buralli of Parma (1247–57).

## Witnesses of Synodality

Franciscans were pioneers in dialogue with nonbelievers, in the exploration of new lands, in the establishments of *Monti di Pietà* financial institutions to protect the poor from usury, in the quest for peace among rival factions, and in the establishment of philosophical and theological dialogue in the universities. The list is endless and is not limited to the spiritual realm.[7]

Francis himself was instrumental in reaching out to nonbelievers. In 1219, when the fifth crusade was fought against the city of Damietta, he famously went to the Holy Land and Egypt to meet the sultan of Egypt, al-Malik al-Kamil. By presenting himself simply as a Christian without any pretense of converting him or waging war on Islam, he succeeded in building up a cordial relationship with the sultan.[8]

The result was the peaceful presence of the Franciscan friars in the Holy Land that is still very much alive today, and in which I participated for sixteen years. Although seemingly a very tense place to live, the Holy Land is also a miracle of peaceful living together. The media are quick to report violence between ethnic groups and tensions among Christians, yet, in doing so, they fail to note the day-to-day ordinary life of the common people. Whether they are Jews, Christians, Muslims, or others, most of these people are peace loving and live together in harmony. The churches practice ecumenical dialogue not simply by sitting down together to discuss theological issues but by living together in the same confined space of the shrines. There is a basis for journeying together that is unique and uncharted. Interestingly, being together on a journey—synodality—extends beyond the Catholic Church here and includes other Christian churches and indeed the three Abrahamic religions at large.

---

7. For these and other developments, see Grado Giovanni Merlo, *In the Name of Saint Francis: History of the Friars Minor and Franciscanism until the Early Sixteenth Century* (St. Bonaventure, NY: Franciscan Institute Publications, 2009).

8. This remarkable feat has been amply studied; see, for example, Jan Hoeberichts, *Francis and the Sultan: Men of Peace* (St. Bonaventure, NY: Franciscan Institute Publications, 2018).

## A Franciscan Approach to Synodality

What should characterize these and other missionary activities, then and now, is a Franciscan spirit of being near to those who suffer, of serving peace instead of hatred, and of fraternity and forgiveness. Or, as Pope Francis described that spirit during the last General Chapter on July 15, 2021:

> That Spirit, who transformed the bitterness of Francis' encounter with the lepers into sweetness of soul and body, is still at work today to give new freshness and energy to each one of you if you will allow yourselves to be stirred by the least of our time. I encourage you to go out to meet the men and women who suffer in soul and body, to offer your humble and fraternal presence, without grand speeches, but making your closeness as lesser brothers felt. To go toward a wounded creation, our common home, which suffers from a distorted exploitation of the earth's goods for the enrichment of a few while creating conditions of misery for many. To go as men of dialogue, seeking to build bridges instead of walls, offering the gift of fraternity and friendship in a world that is struggling to find the path of a common vision. To go forth as men of peace and reconciliation, inviting those who sow hatred, division and violence to conversion of heart, and offering the victims the hope that comes from truth, justice and forgiveness. From these encounters, you will receive an impetus to live the Gospel ever more fully.[9]

One of the more recent insights is that we should collaborate with the laity. In the "Final Document" of the 2021 General Chapter, it states that "in all areas of evangelizing activity, the

---

9. Pope Francis, "Message of the Holy Father to the Participants of the General Chapter of the Order of Friars" (July 15, 2021), https://ofm.org/en/message-of-the-holy-father-to-the-participants-of-the-general-chapter-of-the-order-of-friars-minor.html.

## Witnesses of Synodality

brothers should strive to collaborate with the laity in a spirit of shared mission and synodality."[10]

This quick historical overview suggests, first, that synodality and walking together is not an easy enterprise. The variety of convictions within the Franciscan family has led to tensions and resulted in divisions. Does it suggest that we need to learn to deal better with diversity to realize the ideal of synodality? Should we bear with another more patiently? Should we respect that people may go in different directions within the one body of the church?

This overview suggests that the synodal process is greatly served by a spirit of flexibility and creativity. Just as the Franciscan family has been listening attentively to the signs of the times, especially to the cries of the poor, to social issues, to the plight of immigrants, and just as it has done so in dialogue with nonbelievers and with other religions, so too can and should the church adapt creatively and flexibly to the circumstances it encounters. Interestingly, the Franciscan order is not clerical: one can perfectly well serve the kingdom without ordination. That, too, is a reassuring (and maybe unsettling) message for the church, now that it seeks to embrace a synodal way of proceeding.

## *Laudato Si'*

Saint Francis is probably best known for his love for nature. The *Fioretti*, a collection of devout, largely hagiographic stories, speaks of Francis establishing peace between the wolf of Gubbio and the inhabitants of the town that it was terrorizing; the wolf was to stop his threats, and the townspeople were to feed the wolf.[11] Other stories speak of Francis preaching to the birds, some-

---

10. OFM General Chapter, "Final Document: Mandates and Orientations," 25, in: *Acta Capituli Generalis OFM 2021*, 1118.

11. For the story of Francis and the wolf of Gubbio, see *The Little Flowers of Saint*

## A Franciscan Approach to Synodality

thing that is often depicted in images of Francis. Underlying these anecdotes is a deep awe and wonder of nature—not just animals but nature in general, including clouds, trees, rocks, and rivers.

One of the richest expressions of this profound nature mysticism is the canticle that Francis composed toward the end of his life, and that starts with famous opening words *Laudato Si'*, "praised be [God]." Interestingly, by that time, Francis was virtually blind. Even though he could not behold the beauty of creation with his bodily eyes anymore, he continued his praise to God. The canticle is unique in that it speaks about creatures as being brothers and sisters. Francis praises God for, among other things...

> Brother Sun, who is the day and through whom You give us light;
> Sister Moon and the stars, clear and precious and beautiful;
> Brother Wind and the air, cloudy and serene;
> Sister Water, who is very useful and humble and precious and chaste;
> Brother Fire, through whom You light the night, and he is beautiful and playful and robust and strong;
> Sister Mother Earth, who sustains and governs us, and produces various fruit with coloured flowers and herbs.[12]

Francis even praises God for "Sister Bodily Death from whom no one living can escape."

Thus, the human person engages in relationship with nature. This contrasts with using creation as a tool for self-complacency

---

*Francis*, or *Fioretti*, chapter 21, in Francis of Assisi, *Early Documents* III, 601–3.

12. Francis of Assisi, "Canticle of the Creatures," in Francis of Assisi, *Early Documents* I, 113–14.

## Witnesses of Synodality

or an instrument of exploitation. The human person is part of creation and must enter into dialogue with all creatures. Francis expressed this kind of fraternal relationship with creation as a kind of relation among equals. In other words, creatures are not seen to be inferior to people. In one of his "Admonitions," Francis is very clear regarding this attitude: "All creatures under heaven serve, know and obey their Creator, each according to its own nature, better than you."[13] In the "Salutation of the Virtues," Francis even arrives at speaking about the need to be submissive to creation itself:

> Holy Obedience confounds every corporal and carnal wish, binds its mortified body to obedience of the Spirit and obedience to one's brother, so that it is subject and submissive to everyone in the world, not only to people but to every beast and wild animal as well that they may do whatever they want with it insofar as it has been given to them from above by the Lord.[14]

Pope Francis took up this inspiration by choosing the first words of Francis's canticle for the title of his 2015 encyclical on the care for the environment, a challenge that involves the way we relate to nature as much as our relationships with one another, with God, and with our soul. Yet, Francis of Assisi's inspiration also serves the synodal journey. It suggests that we should not only journey peacefully with one another as Christians (or human beings at large) but with nature, with whom we share the one loving God who is the creator and sustainer of all.

---

13. Francis of Assisi, "Admonition 5," in Francis of Assisi, *Early Documents* I, 131.
14. Francis of Assisi, "A Salutation of the Virtues," in Francis of Assisi, *Early Documents* I, 165.

## Conclusion

This chapter has presented some aspects of Franciscan spirituality, then and now, with the hope that those may provide tools for promoting a synodal lifestyle. First, we have seen that saint Francis radically changed the way church leadership was to be lived, and in fact religious life in general. Instead of thinking hierarchically, Francis promoted lowliness. Francis's companions were to call themselves "minor brothers," and the superiors were to be called "servant." The model was that of Jesus washing the feet of his disciples and stating that he did not come into the world to be served but to serve.

These words and the spirit that they convey do indeed help to build up a synodal church that journeys together. It means that the members of the people of God should not consider themselves better than one another—because of (supposed) moral perfection, orthodoxy, theological or other learning, richness, or for whatever other reason—but humbly and simply as fellow travelers. Similarly, it shall be a great help if clergy and all those in leadership fulfill those roles with the spirit of being servant, *minister*, promoted by Francis of Assisi and indeed by Pope Francis today. A decentralized federal way of governing further contributes to a synodal way of proceeding.

Second, we have seen that the Franciscan family has experienced a fair amount of division, which is both a sad feat of failed unity and a sign of an ongoing search for the best way to live the Franciscan charism. It suggests that a synodal church should champion a culture of searching for the truth rather than possessing it. Also, a synodal church needs to find ways to live unity in diversity, despite mistakes and inner divisions.

Third, Saint Francis insisted that missionaries should first give witness of a fraternal life in humility and simply profess that they are Christians, without insisting upon preaching the gospel. It is certainly helpful for a synodal culture of journeying together to prioritize encountering one another rather than convincing or correcting the other person. As Christians, we should reach out to build bridges based on our humanity, without imposing our own point of view on others. Similarly, from a Franciscan perspective, synodality should include the encounter with people outside our own "bubble," that is, Catholics of other persuasions as well as other Christians, non-Christians, and the world at large. Finally, considering *Laudato Si'* and the Franciscan aspect of mysticism, we should include in our synodal journey listening to nature and caring for our common home.

# Bibliography

Bodo, Murray. *Francis: The Journey and the Dream*. Cincinnati, OH: Franciscan Media, 2022.

Francis, Pope. *Laudato Si'*. Encyclical letter, May 24, 2015. https://www.vatican.va/content/francesco/en/encyclicals.

———. "Message of the Holy Father to the Participants of the General Chapter of the Order of Friars." July 15, 2021. https://ofm.org/en/message-of-the-holy-father-to-the-participants-of-the-general-chapter-of-the-order-of-friars-minor.html.

Francis and Clare of Assisi. *Early Sources*. 4 vols. New York: New City Press, 1999–2001. https://www.franciscantradition.org/early-sources.

Hoeberichts, Jan. *Francis and the Sultan: Men of Peace*. Cincinnati, OH: Franciscan Institute Publications, 2018.

Merlo, Grado Giovanni. I*n the Name of Saint Francis: History of the Friars Minor and Franciscanism until the Early Sixteenth Century*. Cincinnati, OH: Franciscan Institute Publications, 2009.

# 4

# An Ursuline Perspective of Synodality

*Laure Blanchon, OSU, and
Armida Veglio, OSU*

From its beginning, the Company of Saint Ursula, founded in 1535 by Saint Angela Merici in Brescia, has been characterized by a style of participation. What is even more unique is that this participative way of proceeding has been combined with an almost exclusively female leadership. This chapter explores the origins of the Company of Saint Ursula and its Rule—the Ursuline inspiration—followed by two contemporary examples of Ursuline decision-making. How do the insights and tools of the Ursuline tradition enrich the church's current synodal renewal?

Witnesses of Synodality

# The Company of Saint Ursula and Its Rule

## A BRIEF HISTORY

The history of the Company of Saint Ursula starts with Angela Merici (1474–1540). A member of the Third Order of Saint Francis, she lived in the countryside around Desenzano and Salò on Lake Garda in the north of Italy until, in her early forties, she was asked to go to Brescia to comfort a widow who had lost her children. There, in Brescia, she started to meet various people: ordinary townsfolk, important dignitaries, theologians and preachers, artists, and humanists. She became known as a holy woman, whom people sought out for her practical and spiritual wisdom, her prayer and insights into scripture, her advice on matters of reconciliation with relatives, and so on.[1]

Among those who flocked to her were women who wanted a life of consecration to God, without entering a monastery, and whom, from 1532, Angela gathered as future members of "the Company of Saint Ursula." The purpose of the company was to form women who wanted to live a communal life of consecration as "true and virginal spouses of the Son of God," but outside the monastery, without vows, enclosure, or habit.[2] There was no specific apostolate or ministry; rather, they were to continue their previous employment while living in their own homes.

By 1535, Angela finished dictating the Rule of the company

---

1. Cf. Antonio Romano's testimony as rendered in Gabriele Cozzano, *Angela Merici: The Scribe and the Witnesses* (Rome: Roman Union of the Order of Saint Ursula, 2020), 111.

2. See Angela Merici, "Rule of the Company of Saint Ursula," prologue, verse 7, in *Writings, Rule, Counsels, Testaments: Earliest-Known Italian Texts* (Rome: Roman Union of the Order of Saint Ursula, 1995). Quotations from Angela's writings are taken from this publication.

to Gabriele Cozzano, her secretary. It was one of the few rules to be written by a woman and one of the few rules for an organized consecrated life without vows. Two more texts followed: the Counsels, addressed to the local leaders of the company, and the Testament, addressed to the lady governors, or matrons, who were not members as such but dealt with administrative matters and represented the members in society when necessary.

After the Council of Trent (1545–63), the company responded to the need for religious education by engaging in the Schools of Christian Doctrine. From the beginning of the seventeenth century, in response to Trent, most Ursuline communities were congregated and, especially in France, cloistered, yet with permission for the nuns to continue the apostolic dimension of their lives by opening a school. This was the beginning of the Order of Saint Ursula. The apostolate of education then became a key characteristic of Ursuline religious life. At the end of the nineteenth century, in response to an appeal by Pope Leo XIII, sixty-two Ursuline monasteries joined together to form the Roman Union.[3]

## A SPIRITUALITY OF PARTICIPATION

Considering the current synodal processes, it is refreshing to note that the Company of Saint Ursula has been characterized by a process of participation from its earliest days. For example, Angela's secretary, Cozzano, tells us that she talked over her ideas concerning the Rule with other members: "She used to talk things over with them, encouraged them to act, saying that

---

3. For more details, see Marie-Bénédicte Rio, *Elements of Ursuline History and Spirituality* (Rome: Roman Union of the Order of Saint Ursula, 1989); Marie de Chantal Guedre, *Les monastères d'Ursulines sous l'Ancien Régime* (Paris: Saint-Paul, 1960); Marie-Andrée Jégou and Marija Jasna Kogoj, *Roman Union Ursulines: Journey toward Unity, 1900–1926* (Rome: Roman Union of the Order of Saint Ursula, 1999).

## Witnesses of Synodality

it was not she, but the virgins with her who had done it. She used to insist that she was indebted to them, truly indebted."[4]

The participative style materialized further through a strong sense of communion among these women "united together to serve his divine Majesty."[5] Angela emphasized words like *insieme* (together), union, and harmony. The word *insieme* represents a spiritual communion that binds together poor and rich members in a company where all have an equal status.[6] In a society in which classes were strictly divided, this was a strong countercultural witness. At the end of her life, she exhorted local leaders to live in harmony: "My last word to you, by which I implore you even with my blood, is that you live in harmony, united together, all of one heart and one will."[7]

Ursuline governance is also characterized by a participative spirit. The government is (almost) entirely in women's hands, something that was unique at the time. In chapter XI of the Rule, Angela describes the company's government as a government by women, of women, for women. "To govern this Company, it is arranged that four of the most capable virgins of the Company should be elected, and at least four widowed matrons [lady governors], prudent and of honest life, and four mature and experienced men."[8] Importantly, all members were eligible for all government positions, regardless of their social background.

---

4. See Gabriele Cozzano's "Commentary on the Bull of Pope Paul III," in *Angela Merici: Contribution toward a Biography*, ed. Luciani Mariani, Elisa Tarolli and Marie Seynaeve (Milan: Ancora, 1986), 644–56. See also *Angela Merici: The Scribe and the Witnesses*, 73–97.

5. "Rule of the Company of Saint Ursula," prologue, verse 4.

6. For the word *insieme*, see the "Rule of the Company of Saint Ursula," prologue, verse 4; VII, verse 13; XI, verse 14; "Counsels Addressed to the Leaders," V, verse 20; "Last Counsel," verses 1 and 15; "Testament" VII, verse 2; VIII, verses 3 and 5; X, verses 10–12.

7. "Counsels," Last Counsel, verse 1.

8. "Rule of the Company of Saint Ursula," XI, verses 1–3.

## An Ursuline Perspective of Synodality

What is striking is that there is no general superior. The Rule for the company was collegial and synodal.[9]

Regarding the nonmembers who are involved in government, Angela spells out that the lady governors should regularly meet with the leaders to evaluate how the company is being governed. Moreover, they should regularly meet with all the Ursuline members.[10] Four laymen should act as agents for legal matters, if required; they were, in fact, not elected until twenty years after the foundation.

In her Last Legacy to the lady governors, Angela reveals her radical openness to adapt to changing circumstances and the signs of the times:

> Finally, take the greatest care that the good directives given, especially those in the Rule, be most diligently observed. And if, according to times and circumstances, the need arises to make new rules or do something differently, do it prudently and with good advice. And always let your principal recourse be to gather at the feet of Jesus Christ, and there, all of you, with all your daughters, to offer most fervent prayers.[11]

A participative spirit accords well with flexibility concerning the mission. Indeed, the Rule does not specify a particular apostolate or mission. For Angela, the purpose of the company was the formation of the members as spouses of the Son of God and as mediators of salvation and reconciliation in society, for example, by counseling and promoting peace. In the chapter on virginity, she affirms: "Let all our words, actions and behaviour

---

9. Angela was elected "principal mother" in 1537 for practical reasons. An inheritance had been left to the company, but there was no legal representative to accept it.

10. "Testament," Seventh and Eighth Legacies.

11. "Testament of Mother Sister Angela Bequeathed to the Lady-Governors," Last Legacy, verses 1-4.

## Witnesses of Synodality

always be for the instruction and edification of those who have dealings with us, always have charity burning in our hearts."[12] In the Fifth Counsel, she tells the leaders that their daughters should "seek to spread peace and concord where they are."[13]

## Two Contemporary Examples

The participative style that marked the life of the first members of the Company of Saint Ursula is still present in the life of Ursuline communities today. The practice of co-responsibility, communal discernment, and common decision-making characterizes both the functioning of local communities and the way of proceeding of the Roman Union. Synodal dynamics form the framework of Ursuline community and missionary life. However, it is also fair to acknowledge that it is not that simple and that these participative procedures always require a learning process. They require evaluation and conversion so that they can be practiced more authentically.

With the help of two real cases, we will now consider how these participative procedures work concretely and explore how synodal procedures were implemented ("the facts") and what we might learn from them ("an analysis of the process") for a synodal church.

### BUYING A NEW CAR

#### The Facts

This case concerns our community of nine sisters in a small rural town without public transportation. Due to a car accident,

---

12. "Rule of the Company of Saint Ursula," IX, verses 21–22.
13. "Counsels," V, verse 16.

the community lost one of two cars. Initially, we decided to try living with one car. After a few months, the community evaluated the decision and concluded that it was not possible to continue with this option. Significantly, several sisters needed frequent access to healthcare, which, in a rural area, necessitates a car. Moreover, the car was required for pastoral work covering a vast area of over ten surrounding rural parishes. It was also used for doing the shopping for the community. Together, we resolved to buy a new car. To decide what type of car was needed, the community shared with one another each person's needs. Gradually, a profile of a car emerged. Finally, after considering the financial aspect, the community established a budget.

Our community enjoys the help of a lay volunteer to maintain the buildings and cars. Based on what we shared with him regarding our needs, he prepared an overview of the various cars that were offered for sale on the internet and at local car dealerships. This helped the community to be realistic in their reflection and discernment. The overview specified technical information on contemporary ecological challenges, among other things. The document was shared with all the sisters.

After everyone had read the document, we met to discuss and discern together. Each sister could share her personal needs and state her opinion regarding which car would best serve the community. Gradually, a consensus emerged, and a decision was made. The lay volunteer was entrusted with buying the car.

Reflecting on this process of communal listening and discernment now, we realize that we had not given the same weight to the various aspects of the process. In particular, we had not sufficiently considered the needs of the most vulnerable members of the community. Consequently, we have learned that listening to everyone is an ongoing process.

# Witnesses of Synodality

## *An Analysis of the Process*

What can we learn from this first case study? What are the building blocks for a more synodal church?

For a start, we went through a process that lasted several months. Synodality is slow. Our community wanted to adapt to "times and circumstances,"[14] and to do this, we experimented for a few weeks and then reviewed our first decision. Synodality involves *trying out* and *evaluating*. Once we knew that the community wanted a second car, we took time for several conversations so that we could move forward *together* and gradually refine the decision. Synodality is done *together*. In our discernment, the community looked for what was good, both for the entire community and for each sister individually, in a fruitful tension between "all together" and "each person individually" characteristic of Angela.[15] The community asked for the help of a competent person on the technical and administrative aspects, keeping the Merician tradition of asking for the help of laypeople. Synodality uses external expertise.

## REWRITING THE CONSTITUTIONS

## *The Facts*

The 2019 General Chapter voted for rewriting the Constitutions, specifying that this writing process is to be prepared by a formation process that involves all the members.[16] The chapter explicitly requested to "involve all of the Institute's sisters in a process of consultation and dialogue in view of writing new

---

14. "Testament," Last Legacy, verse 2.
15. Cf. "Counsels," Prologue, verse 11.
16. Cf. Ursulines of the Roman Union, "General Chapter 2019," section "Road Map—Decisions."

## An Ursuline Perspective of Synodality

Constitutions."[17] The following year, the prioress general and her council set up the Constitutions Commission in which they appointed sisters from different backgrounds and with various expertise.

Once the commission was established, it needed to decide how to collaborate and how to carry out the consultation with the members. First, the commission wrote a prayer to entrust ourselves to the Spirit. It then developed an eighteen-month formation in the theology of religious life to shape a common ethos across the Roman Union. The commission regularly selected theological texts that it sent out with an invitation to personal reflection and community conversations; it also asked the community to send back some echoes. The feedback helped the commission to choose its ongoing selection of texts to send out.

After this first phase, which focused on formation, the second phase was about identifying the elements that were essential for the new Constitutions, according to the canonical norms. The commission invited the sisters to start a process of discernment and synthesis that involved five stages. The first stage consisted of personal discernment: What are the essential elements for each chapter? In the second stage, communities and groups engaged in conversation and common discernment: Which five elements are essential for each chapter? Third, the lists with the elements that had been discerned communally were sent to the commission. Fourth, the commission then processed the results, by both synthesizing and discerning, taking into consideration the variety of contexts: What had emerged? Finally, an Enlarged General Council discerned the outcomes and then decided what were the essential elements that needed to be integrated into the new Constitutions. The method consisted of a study of the

---

17. Ursulines of the Roman Union, "General Chapter 2019," section "Road Map—Orientations."

## Witnesses of Synodality

outcomes, a calm conversation to better understand the various contexts, and a search for a consensus on determining the necessary content of the chapters.

The process ended with the creation of a document including the "Essential Elements" to enable the Constitutions Commission to start drafting the new Constitutions.

With the first draft completed (in September 2023), the following step is that the draft will be sent to all the sisters for personal and communal discernment. With their feedback, a second draft will be prepared. Finally, an Extraordinary General Chapter will be called to work toward a final version and then to vote on the text.

## An Analysis of the Process

Although the process is still ongoing, a couple things stand out. First, the whole process is rooted in prayer to the Holy Spirit. Synodality is a *prayerful* process. All the sisters are involved in a discernment process that goes back and forth between various levels: personal input, local conversations (in community or other groups), the work of the ad hoc commission, and the joint deliberations by those who hold authority. Synodality is *inclusive* and *circular*. The conversation processes include extended periods of listening to one another, which makes it possible for people to transcend their own views and see beyond their own context. By broadening our perspectives, the final position is more inclusive and acknowledges everyone's situation, including those of minorities. Synodality requires being ready to change one's views, and one must *include minorities*. Finally, note that the decision process has two dimensions: the maturing process of *decision-making*, in which everyone is actively involved, and the *decision-taking* by those with major leadership roles.[18] The brotherly (or here, sisterly) aspect—as sisters we are all equal in the process—goes together with a hierarchical principle. Ecclesial realities such as the church at large and the Roman Union are not democracies but human-divine realities in which these two principles are combined. Synodality cannot function without *leadership*.

## THE URSULINE SYNODAL WAY OF LIVING

Based on these two cases, let us highlight a couple of characteristics of Ursuline synodality. In our communities, there is a desire to practice synodality both in day-to-day decisions and in major occurrences in the Roman Union. It is a matter of learning by doing. This includes trial and error, adjusting, rethinking—and great determination throughout the process. The goal is to initiate synodal processes in all areas and to take the time to develop them gradually.

The determination in choosing synodality is rooted in the *insieme* emphasized by Angela. The aim is to construct together what concerns all and not to impose a decision taken in isolation by a given authority—the community leadership team, the prioress, the project steering team, and so on. Loyalty to this *insieme* calls on those managing the processes to ensure that no one gets forgotten and, therefore, that special attention is given to the most vulnerable. Often this "all" involves not just the community of the sisters but also the local ecclesial community. It is important, therefore, to include laypeople in the decision-making process and to intensify their collaboration.

Angela's invitation to adapt is part of the ordinary ethos of Ursuline religious and educational communities: "If, according to times and circumstances, the need arises to make new

---

18. Alphonse Borras, *Communion ecclésiale et synodalité. Comprendre la synodalité selon le pape François* (Paris: Éditions CLD, 2018), 104–5.

# Witnesses of Synodality

rules or do something differently, do it prudently and with good advice."[19] The experience of synodal processes is permeated with this spirit. It involves discerning with freedom what is appropriate to continue and what to let go, adapting according to times and circumstances, moving forward step-by-step to find the right path with both action and reflection in a process of trying out, evaluating, adjusting, and taking the next step.

Ursuline discernment is a spiritual experience rooted in an openness to the Holy Spirit and an active and prolonged listening to the situation and to persons, to take into account the whole reality and to have a profound respect for the uniqueness of individuals without losing a sense of the whole body.

This fidelity to the Spirit, to each person, and to all together ensures that we value "diversity in communion" within the synodal processes.[20] Welcoming disagreements and differing points of view, and listening to them, allows for a broader view to mature. This broader view will incorporate elements that were initially not sufficiently noticed. The best of each person is gathered, appreciated, and brought into dialogue with the best of the other participants. Gradually, a rich communion amid diversity ripens. The synodal, communal "we" is, therefore, more than simply the sum of its parts, for this synodal communion incorporates a wealth of relationships.[21] Imagining synodality as a union in symphonic diversity gives great weight both to the contribution of each person and to the collaboration between the various members. In the *insieme*, everyone is precious and unique. If one person is missing, the entire body is wounded and weakened.

---

19. "Testament," Last Legacy, verse 2.

20. This perspective implements the principles presented by Pope Francis in the *Apostolic Exhortation Evangelii Gaudium* (2013), 221–37: time is greater than space, unity prevails over conflict, realities are more important than ideas, the whole is greater than the parts and also greater than the sum of its parts.

21. Based on Agnès Desmazières, *Le dialogue pour surmonter la crise* (Paris: Salvator, 2020), 144.

## Conclusion

At the end of this journey through the Ursuline tradition, what should we keep in mind for the church's synodal transformation? First, the very old Merician *insieme* tradition leads to a concern for the inclusion of all and the appreciation of each person's contribution. In a church where the emphasis is often on hierarchy—in Angela's time just like ours—it is highly valuable to emphasize the contribution of all and the value of each baptized person.

Second, the *insieme* invites us to avoid elitism whereby everything is in the hands of the superior, as well as the closed circuit of speaking only among ourselves as Ursulines. Instead, we should "enlarge the space of our tent" (Isa 54:2) by manifold collaborations and partnerships that involve all the sisters as well as laypeople and sisters. To do so, we need procedures that make the most of common *decision-making* while respecting that *decision-taking* is the responsibility of the hierarchical authority, be it a religious superior or a bishop.

Finally, the implementation of a participative style is supported by various elements that go together and strengthen one other. These include listening to the Spirit; deep and slow listening to each person and to the whole body; ensuring that everyone has access to information; engaging in processes of discernment, adapting to circumstances and people, and learning from experience; and allowing things to settle and take time to mature.

## Bibliography

Borras, Alphonse. *Communion ecclésiale et synodalité: Comprendre la synodalité selon le pape François*. Paris: Éditions CLD, 2018.
Cozzano, Gabriele. *Angela Merici: The Scribe and the Witnesses*. Rome: Roman Union of the Order of Saint Ursula, 2020.

## Witnesses of Synodality

———. "Commentary on the Bull of Pope Paul III." In *Angela Merici: Contribution toward a Biography*. Edited by Luciani Mariani, Elisa Tarolli and Marie Seynaeve, 644–56. Milan: Ancora, 1986.

Desmazières, Agnès. *Le dialogue pour surmonter la crise*. Paris: Salvator, 2020.

Guedre, Marie de Chantal. *Les monastères d'Ursulines sous l'Ancien Régime*. Paris: Saint-Paul, 1960.

Jégou, Marie-Andrée, and Marija Jasna Kogoj. *Roman Union Ursulines: Journey toward Unity, 1900–1926*. Rome: Roman Union of the Order of Saint Ursula, 1999.

Merici, Angela. *Writings, Rule, Counsels, Testaments: Earliest-Known Italian Texts*. Rome: Roman Union of the Order of Saint Ursula, 1995.

Rio, Marie-Bénédicte. *Elements of Ursuline History and Spirituality*. Rome: Roman Union of the Order of Saint Ursula, 1989.

# 5

# Common Discernment and the Founding of the Jesuits

*Jos Moons, SJ*[*]

The church is sometimes seen as an institute of certainty, and it sometimes presents itself as such, but a synodal church is more like a seeker, wanting to learn and eager to hear what the Spirit is saying to it in our time. Moreover, a synodal church is primarily a community of fellow pilgrims. We all have wisdom to share and wisdom to receive. Clearly, the church has a hierarchical leadership structure, but bishops should also listen and learn before they decide. Who knows if the Spirit speaks through the "ordinary" faithful?[1]

One of the key problems with this notion of church is finding direction. How does one know if a new idea is of the Spirit or not, and if an old idea is still valid? As synodality encourages people to speak out, the problem becomes worse. Various

---

1. For a broad presentation of synodality, see Jos Moons, "A Comprehensive Introduction to Synodality: Reconfiguring Ecclesiology and Ecclesial Practice," *Annals of Theology* 69, no. 2 (2022): 73–93.

ideas—some of which used to be considered taboo—are now on the table. What is the Spirit telling us here? To answer that question, traditional Catholic approaches need updating. If the Spirit is speaking here and now, we must complement reaching back to the past to scripture and tradition with reading the signs of the times. And if we are primarily fellow pilgrims, then we must pair trusting in the hierarchy with consultation and transparency.

This chapter revisits the very beginning of the Society of Jesus (the Jesuits) with a particular interest in how the first Jesuits dealt with conflicting views. The so-called *Deliberatio Primorum Patrum* (Deliberation of the first fathers) describes how the first companions proceeded when they realized that they disagreed about the future.[2] One of the outcomes of their common discernment was to adopt the vow of obedience to a superior. Although the *Deliberatio*, therefore, is not really a model for current Jesuit governance, it can be instructive for our synodal journey in various ways.

## The *Deliberatio* and the Founding of the Jesuits

During his time of studies in Paris, the Basque Ignatius of Loyola (1491–1556) gathered a group of "friends in the Lord" who studied theology, served the poor, and grew in the spiritual life. In 1534, they took vows in Montmartre (Paris), promising chastity, poverty, and a journey to the Holy Land to preach

---

2. For a solid presentation of the text, see Jules J. Toner, "The Deliberation That Started the Jesuits: A Commentary on the *Deliberatio Primorum Patrum*; Newly Translated with a Historical Introduction," *Studies in the Spirituality of Jesuits* 4 (1974): 179–212. See also Joseph Conwell, "Deliberaciones 1539," in *Diccionario de Espiritualidad Ignaciana*, ed. Javier Melloni et al. (Bilbao: Mensajero, 2007), 549–53. For critical questions, cf. Ladislas Orsy, "Toward a Theological Evaluation of Communal Discernment," *Studies in the Spirituality of Jesuits* 5 (1973): 139–88.

## Common Discernment and the Founding of the Jesuits

the gospel. When it turned out that the early companions—ten in number—were not able to go to the Holy Land as they had vowed, they offered themselves, in 1538, to the pope for any mission that he would see fit. As they would be missioned to different places, the companions came together to discuss whether they wanted to stay united as a group, and if so, how? For almost three months, the companions considered these questions. Afterward, a record of the meeting, the *Deliberatio Primorum Patrum*, was drawn up.

A relatively short document divided into nine paragraphs, the *Deliberatio* starts with briefly setting the scene and then presents two different types of common discernment. The starting point is a clear disagreement on how to proceed. For although "all had one mind and heart in seeking God's gracious and perfect will according to the scope of our vocation," the *Deliberatio* acknowledges that "regarding the more readily effective and more fruitful ways of achieving God's will for ourselves and others, we held diverse views" (§ 1).[3] The author of the *Deliberatio* seems somewhat uneasy about this. He refers to the geographical backgrounds—"some of us were French, others Spanish, Savoyards, or Portuguese"—and further explains that this is part of the human condition: "No one ought to wonder that this diversity of views should be found among us, spiritually infirm and feeble men," as the apostles and other holy men were also known to have had different views (§ 1).

Interestingly, the solution is not to leave the group but to double one's effort to find a solution. The companions search for a method. "Since we did hold different judgments, we were eagerly on the watch to discover some unobstructed way along which we might advance together and all of us offer ourselves as a holocaust to our God, in whose praise, honor, and glory we would yield our all" (§ 1). On the one hand, they trust in God,

---

3. All quotes are taken from Toner, "Deliberation That Started the Jesuits."

## Witnesses of Synodality

who "is so kind and generous that he never denies his good Spirit to anyone who petitions him in humility and simplicity of heart" (§ 1). Simultaneously, they dedicate themselves more fervently to prayer and Mass and to "pondering, meditating, and prayerfully searching into" the question at hand (§ 2). In addition, they would share their thoughts, with the objective to identify "the more powerful reasons" and to embrace those together (§ 2). Finally, if unity could not be achieved, a majority vote was to be decisive.

Resolving the first question—would they stay united, or not?—seems to have been relatively straightforward: "In the end we established the affirmative side of the question" (§ 3). They decide to stay united to appreciate that God had gathered them in the past, and because it would help to achieve their future goal, that is, to serve God and humankind. That clarity is greeted as a gift of God—"it was solely what our Lord inspired" (§ 3)—although it has also resulted from the method that they have followed.

When the second question—on adding the vow of obedience—proved much more difficult, another method was designed. To increase the chances of success, the companions opted for a similar yet more rigorously structured process. Participants would focus for one day on the advantages of obedience and for another day on its disadvantages. In addition, to grow further in inner freedom, they would not speak about the matter among themselves, and they would consider the matter as if they were looking at it from the outside (§ 6).[4] As with the

---

4. Here one recognizes instructions from what Ignatius calls the third "time" for making choices, such as listing arguments in favor or against, thinking them over well, and deliberating where one's reason is moved to most; or wondering what advice I would give to a friend. See the section on the so-called Election, *Spiritual Exercises*, nos. 169–89, esp. 178–83 and 185. Interestingly, these instructions are meant to help when another, more affective approach doesn't work—as is clearly the case here.

first method, they would share their thoughts in the evening, with the aim of identifying the more important considerations. With the new method, the process remained laborious. "During many days, from this side and that, we worked over a mass of data related to the resolution of our problem; we examined and weighed the more forceful and important reasons and took time as usual for prayer, meditation, and reflection" (§ 8). Yet, "by the Lord's help," a shared conviction was reached, namely, to adopt the vow of obedience. After that, it seems that other questions were treated (cf. § 9). The very last words of the *Deliberatio* note that "all our business was completed and terminated in a spirit of gladness and harmony" (§ 9). Here we seem to return to the opening words, "all having one mind and heart in seeking God's gracious and perfect will according to the scope of our vocation," yet this time without opposing viewpoints in realizing that.

## The Importance of Method

How can the *Deliberatio* be instructive for synodality? In the first place, the *Deliberatio* stands out for its constructive way of dealing with opposing viewpoints and tensions, namely, to search for a method that helps the process move forward. Tensions are considered normal. When it comes to synodality, we should therefore put our energy not in avoiding tensions but in converting them into a *discernment* process. Maybe one should even say that, for synodality, disagreements and tensions are a good sign, for they indicate that we're truly searching.

Arguably, this is more than pragmatic flexibility; rather, it points at deep faith in God. It is indeed a core conviction of the Ignatian tradition that God interacts with human beings and will let them find out "his will," or, in modern language, how best to live and what best to choose. Ignatius's own spiritual experience

## Witnesses of Synodality

and his experience in accompanying others have made him aware that "the Creator works directly with the creature, and the creature with the Creator and Lord," as he puts it in the *Spiritual Exercises*.[5] When we cannot clearly see where God is leading us, we may need to think of a better way of exploring and discerning that.

That is what happens at the beginning of the *Deliberatio*, when the companions realize that they hold different views. While one needs to stick to method, one also needs to be flexible. Therefore, when the first companions discovered that their initial way of proceeding did not lead to a conclusion for their second question, they once more reconsidered their method. "When we had persisted in prayer and thought for many days without hitting upon any satisfactory resolution of our uncertainty, we put our hope in the Lord and started to cast about for better ways of working out such a resolution" (§ 5). Thus, the *Deliberatio* suggests that one must be flexible when circumstances require.

Ironically, the *Deliberatio* itself should not be absolutized either. Since the second question on taking a vow of obedience was answered positively, time-consuming common discernment processes like that of the *Deliberatio* are less needed. Indeed, one of the meanings of the vow of obedience is that it promotes missionary efficiency. To the extent that the provincial superior (and, to a lesser extent, the general superior and the local superior) takes the decisions, the other companions are free to carry out their mission. Of course, this does not rule out that Jesuits also have a fair (and healthy) personal responsibility that also involves discernment.

At the same time, the insights underlying the *Deliberatio*—namely, that God interacts with each person—remain valid. Therefore, various practices have been developed to consider

---

5. *Spiritual Exercises*, no. 15. Therefore, Ignatius strongly discourages spiritual directors from influencing the outcome of a given discernment—they should only help the process. Cf. *Spiritual Exercises*, no. 16.

## Common Discernment and the Founding of the Jesuits

God's possible communication through nonsuperiors. At an interval of about ten to fifteen years, Jesuits gather in General Congregations to elect a general superior (in a peculiar process that involves *murmuratio* and voting) and to set out the course for the next period, not unlike chapters in other religious orders.[6] Moreover, Jesuit superiors are supposed to regularly take council from a small group of advisors, the so-called consult. And most importantly, as one of his most important tasks, a provincial superior must listen to "the soul" of his companions once a year, so that he knows his people, their desires, their strengths and weaknesses, and their sense of vocation; this practice is called the "account of conscience." Finally, since the 1970s, common discernment (also called communal discernment or discernment in common) has been promoted.

What does this suggest for synodality? Inspired by the *Deliberatio*, we could normalize the tensions that have emerged in the current synodal process and affirm that one can be searching God's will amid opposing points of view and tensions. The best way to deal with tensions is to appreciate them as part of the process and to design a method that facilitates prayerful discernment. This involves, for example, specifying what question we are treating and determining an outline for a spiritual process. In this regard, the *Instrumentum Laboris*'s clear presentation of topics and questions and the outline of a method of "Conversations in the Spirit" is certainly promising.

In addition, the above suggests that we should relativize any specific method for synodality. During their discernment process, the first companions adapted their initial method, so that the *Deliberatio* itself does not offer one single method. Moreover, since that time, Jesuit governance usually includes a superior. A variety of methods have been developed, all of which

---

6. *Murmuratio* is Latin and means here a process of confidential one-on-one conversations about suitable candidates for becoming general superior between those participating in a General Congregation.

were different from the *Deliberatio*. What has remained is a practice that sought to balance efficient, hierarchical leadership and various forms of common discernment.

## Essential Practices and Virtues

In the previous section, we focused on method in a general sense. This may have given the impression that, as far as content is concerned, common discernment is a matter of "just" sharing one's point of view. In fact, common discernment supposes quite specific practices and virtues, most of which are only visible between the lines of the *Deliberatio*. Let us now elaborate on a couple of those practices and virtues.[7]

First, the *Deliberatio*—and discernment in general—supposes inner freedom or, in Ignatian language, "indifference." To see God's will clearly, one needs to be ready to give up any "favorites" (or "attachments," in Ignatian jargon), in the form of one's conviction, feeling, thought, or plan. Instead, one ought to contemplate the possibility that God may be found also, or more so, in another conviction, feeling, thought, or plan. (Without such inner freedom, the first companions would all have stayed with their initial point of view so that a conclusion would have been impossible.)

Synodality supposes a similar freedom. A more psychological term for such freedom is "openness." Pope Francis regularly encourages us to be open to "the surprises of the Holy Spirit" and to the Spirit's "newness." Openness, however, is not often evident in the Roman Catholic Church, which is known more for its closed certainty than for its openness. Church leadership

---

7. For an accessible account of discernment, see Nikolaas Sintobin, *Trust Your Feelings: Learning How to Make Wise Choices* (New York: Paulist Press, 2023). For a scholarly account, see Jules J. Toner, *A Commentary on Saint Ignatius's Rules for the Discernment of Spirits: A Guide to the Principles and Practice* (St. Louis: The Institute of Jesuit Sources, 1982).

## Common Discernment and the Founding of the Jesuits

has tended to promote labeling different views as "unorthodox," and therefore rejecting them, thereby ruling out openness. Brothers and sisters on both the conservative and liberal sides of the spectrum who have an absolute certainty about how to proceed suffer from a similar lack of freedom. Whatever form certainty takes, a lack of inner freedom seriously impedes synodal common discernment.

Second, the *Deliberatio*—and again, discernment in general—supposes a capacity for spiritual self-reflection. From an Ignatian perspective, this involves both a rational and an affective dimension. The first companions were supposed to think about "reasons" and to identify "weightier" reasons. To do so, they prayed, pondered, meditated, and reflected. The point was to identify how God and humankind were best served. In that light, clearly, not all thoughts were as important. Moreover, in dealing with the question of obedience, they decided to structure their thoughts, distinguishing between advantages and disadvantages. In terms of human capacities, this supposes that one has access to one's thoughts and that one can reflect on them.

Discernment also engages one's affective capacities. In the famous "Rules for Discernment," Ignatius speaks about "the various movements produced in the soul" that one has to evaluate.[8] For this, he suggests considering the inner aftertaste and the outcome of a given experience, feeling, or thought. Are there hints of the kingdom of God? Or, with Paul, does one note "love, joy, peace, patience, kindness, generosity, faithfulness, gentleness, and self-control" (Gal 5:22–23)? Does it promote the kingdom of God—that is, does it increase love, joy, peace, patience, kindness, generosity, faithfulness, gentleness…? Typical examples are the spiritual experience of a beautiful Easter vigil or a silent

---

[8]. For these Rules, see the *Spiritual Exercises*, nos. 313–36, here quoted from Ignatius of Loyola, *Personal Writings*, ed. Joseph A. Munitiz and Philip Endean (London: Penguin Books, 1996). Cf. the full title: "Rules by which to perceive and understand to some extent the various movements produced in the soul: The good that they may be accepted and the bad that they may be rejected."

## Witnesses of Synodality

prayer in a church, mild thoughts about the faults of others, active charity or generosity, intellectual simplicity and clarity that answers a question satisfactorily, thankfulness, and wonder. Ignatius welcomes such experiences, feelings, or thoughts as consolation: they indicate that we are on the right path. The opposite holds true for experiences, feelings, or thoughts with a bitter, cold, distressing, hard, superficial aftertaste or outcome.[9]

Thus, spiritual discernment is simultaneously an affective and rational process. Whatever one senses spiritually, one needs to scrutinize—discern—intellectually. And, vice versa, any thoughts on what best serves the kingdom should also give us the *sense* that this is indeed so.

Two more crucial aspects that cannot be elaborated here are the following. Discernment is done in the context of a prayerful familiarity with Christ, an attitude of service and humility after the example of Christ, and trust in the Holy Spirit. Moreover, dialogue with others is both helpful to articulate one's sentiments and thoughts and to unmask illusions.

The practices and virtues listed so far are required for personal discernment. In the case of common discernment, these need to be complemented by more social practices and virtues. Although unmentioned in the *Deliberatio*, they can be identified by reading between the lines. Moreover, they are part of any modern participative decision-making process. One needs independence to be able to "own" one's position. One needs tolerance to bear the fact that others have different views. One needs to be able to delay judgment and to keep one's mouth shut to listen. One needs interest to be open to receiving the views of others, as well as receptivity, so that one may learn from others. Therefore, one also needs to be able to spend time alone and together fruitfully. One needs patience.

---

9. Examples taken from Jos Moons, *The Art of Spiritual Direction: A Guide to Ignatian Practice* (Mahwah, NJ: Paulist Press, 2021).

## Common Discernment and the Founding of the Jesuits

What does this mean for synodality? Considering the *Deliberatio*, synodality supposes well-formed participants. They should be solid, mature people who know themselves well. They should be in touch with their thoughts and feelings and be able to reflect on those. They should be able to relate to others and be both confident to "own" a certain position and humble enough to reconsider it. They should relate to Christ in prayer as well as in service. Once again, these virtues have not always been a priority in the formation of Christians, in general, or clergy, in particular. As they are crucial for common discernment, developing formation programs is of the highest importance.

## Conclusion

The *Deliberatio* could be seen as a "good practice" that confirms, informs, and relativizes synodality. It *confirms* synodality by showing that it is possible to grow from disagreement to agreement, and thereby encourages all those who are committed to a more inclusive and participative church.

As a good practice, the *Deliberatio* also *informs* synodality by suggesting what may help us to progress. In this chapter, we have underlined the importance of method and the crucial significance of a quite specific set of virtues and practices. Ideally, a person who dreams of synodal ways of proceeding should be able to identify, reflect on, and manage one's sentiments and thoughts. Social skills allow one to interact with others who are different or who hold different views. A mixture of self-confidence and humility allows for sharing one's views with an ability to learn from others. An active prayerful relationship with God that goes with an attitude of service after the example of Christ provides our actions with a Christian depth.

Finally, our exploration of the *Deliberatio* invites us to *relativize* any specific method for synodality. The aim is to search for wisdom and God's will, and to do so together. Method is no more than a means for that and should, therefore, be treated with flexibility.

## Bibliography

Conwell, Joseph. "Deliberaciones 1539." In *Diccionario de Espiritualidad Ignaciana*, edited by Javier Melloni et al., 549–53. Bilbao: Mensajero, 2007.

Moons, Jos. "A Comprehensive Introduction to Synodality: Reconfiguring Ecclesiology and Ecclesial Practice." *Annals of Theology* 69, no. 2 (2022): 73–93.

Orsy, Ladislas. "Toward a Theological Evaluation of Communal Discernment." *Studies in the Spirituality of Jesuits* 5 (1973): 139–88.

Sintobin, Nikolaas. *Trust Your Feelings: Learning How to Make Wise Choices*. Mahwah, NJ: Paulist Press, 2023.

Toner, Jules J. *A Commentary on Saint Ignatius's Rules for the Discernment of Spirits: A Guide to the Principles and Practice*. St. Louis: The Institute of Jesuit Sources, 1982.

———. "The Deliberation That Started the Jesuits: A Commentary on the *Deliberatio Primorum Patrum*; Newly Translated with a Historical Introduction." *Studies in the Spirituality of Jesuits* 4 (1974): 179–212.

\* I am grateful to Philip Endean, SJ, and Nikolaas Sintobin, SJ, for their feedback on earlier drafts of this text.

# 6

# Community Discernment amid Violence

## The Monks of Tibhirine

*Marie-Dominique Minassian*

"We didn't elect you to make our decisions for us," says a brother to his prior in Xavier Beauvois's film, *Of Gods and Men*.[1] The movie familiarized the world with the story of the seven monks of Tibhirine who were kidnapped and assassinated in Algeria in 1996. The community, however, functioned quite differently in reality from what the quote suggests. The writings of the members of the community reveal a mature practice of communal decision-taking, even under the pressure of events. This chapter presents their story as an inspiring example for a synodal church. First, we consider how the monks dealt with the difficult questions with which the growing violence confronted

---

1. Originally *Des hommes et des dieux*, winner of the Grand Prix du Jury at the 2010 Cannes Film Festival.

them and conclude with some general considerations for creating a synodal church.

# The Chronicle of a Discernment (1993–1996)

The monks of Tibhirine had shared the country's turbulent history since their arrival in Algeria in 1938. They pursued a monastic life through precarious circumstances that they embraced with faith, hope, and charity. Although the Christian community had already drastically been reduced, after the War of Independence (1954–62) the country was about to turn into a bloodbath. The monks tried to make sense of these events and to discern God's will.

## DECEMBER 1, 1993: AN ULTIMATUM

It started with the stolen elections of 1991 that triggered a violent civil war between the Islamic Salvation Front (FIS), who had won the elections, and the army. In December 1993, the violence extended to all foreigners, who were ordered by the Armed Islamic Group (GIA) to leave the country. A number of religious congregations decided to return to Europe. Others chose to remain in solidarity with those whose daily lives they had chosen to embrace. Although the brothers wrote reassuring letters to their families in Europe, Brother Christian, the prior, began to draft his will.

As soon as the ultimatum expired, the ongoing killing of foreigners began. On a spiritual retreat a few days after the ultimatum, Jesuit father Sanson invited the monks to think about their personal responsibility—to the point of accepting death—and their ecclesial responsibility, in terms of remaining present to non-Christians.

## Community Discernment amid Violence

On December 14, 1993, twelve Croatian workmen were slaughtered on a nearby building site. It deeply affected the brothers, who knew the men well and used to meet them on major religious feasts. The monks clearly saw that, in these dire times, it was important to help one another; there was a growing desire to strengthen community bonds. The minutes of the community exchanges and their personal notes show that the words from liturgy resonated strongly. The frequency of community meetings increased, with two questions imposing themselves: Whether to stay or leave? What signs of hope were there, in prayer or otherwise?

In preparation of a decision, the prior suggested two series of considerations. First, he recalled that they had taken a vow of a "monastic lifestyle" and grounded the reflection in that vocation. He then recalled the specifics of their work and service to their neighbors: the land, the dispensary, various partnerships, friendly relationships with locals, their prayerful presence, their moral and material support to the poorest, and so on. As the situation developed, the prior formulated specific questions for the meetings. The monks also considered their neighbors (how would they feel if they left?), the ambiguity of the situation (flight or suicide—for staying would be suicidal), and the overwhelming force of fear.

## DECEMBER 24, 1993: ARMED "VISITORS"

In December, an armed group suddenly turned up at the monastery, seriously putting the brothers to the test. Their leader was the one to whom the slaughter of the Croatians was attributed. He called for "the pope of this place," meaning, the prior. Arguing that the monastery was "a place of peace," Brother Christian got the group to leave its enclosure, but not without intense dialogue between the two leaders. Two years later, Brother Christian recounted,

## Witnesses of Synodality

> To me, he was unarmed. We were face to face. He presented his three demands and three times I was able to say no, or "not like that." He then said, "you do not have a choice"; I responded, "yes, I do have a choice." Not only because I was the guardian of my brothers, but also because in fact I was the guardian of this brother who was there in front of me, and who had to be able to discover in himself something other than what he had become.[2]

The prior's amazing resolve awoke the man's hidden humanity, and he finally left the brothers safe and sound. This reveals both Brother Christian's inner freedom and his thoughtfulness under those circumstances.

## END OF DECEMBER 1993: AN INTENSE REFLECTION

The community was deeply impacted by this visit; there was a before and an after. Community meetings became almost a daily affair. The notes that were taken bear witness to an ever more intensified relationship to the Word of God, the fraternal life, and the events in their surroundings.[3] The prior moderated the conversations and asked each person what gave them peace.

The monks were aware that their decisions affected the local church. Henri Teissier, the bishop, joined the community on December 27. Recalling that the mission of the whole church is to be "at this place a gospel of peace," he shared the question: "How can we prepare for the future?" The brothers considered leaving gradually by first sending three brothers to Europe.

---

2. Christian de Chergé, "Recollection, March 8, 1996," in *L'invincible espérance* (Paris: Bayard, 1997), 309.

3. Thomas Georgeon, "Donner sa vie pour la gloire de T'aimer: Tibhirine ou un chemin communautaire vers le martyre," *Collectanea Cisterciensia* 68 (2006): 76–104.

## Community Discernment amid Violence

They were also attentive to other voices, considering those of the guard and his family, the associates working with them, the neighbors, and the Wilaya authorities and the Christians who relied on them. The parish priest of Médéa and Cardinal Duval, archbishop emeritus of Algiers, expressed their closeness to the brothers, with the latter recommending constancy and firmness.

### EARLY 1994: A GROWING CLARITY

At the end of 1993, the monks converged around an option of simplicity:

> Continue to give thanks
> for the landscape,
> the small daily insights,
> the simple relationships with neighbours,
> the present as "ETERNAL."[4]

In the following days, the monks encouraged one another with great openness. The minutes of the community meetings spoke about the resolve to "tell each other all the SIGNS we have received, that take on providential meaning and are the confirmation of a CALLING." These translate into symbolic gestures to the outside world such as "re-open the chapel (it is God's house)."

A brief encounter with a neighbor also nurtured hope. "I said: 'we're like a bird sitting on a branch.' Response: 'No, you are the branch...we are the bird. Don't cut down the tree—the bird won't have anywhere to land!'"

Confronted with life in a community reduced in numbers and faced with the possibility of emotional low tide, the monks

---

4. Brother Christian's minutes of the community exchanges, Atlas archives. All the following quotations are taken from these notes.

formulated concrete intentions: "Greater PATIENCE, with ourselves, with others and with God too! Humour helps! An effort of accuracy with where one needs to be."

## SPRING 1994: LIVING EVENTS *TOGETHER*

Daily life soon resumed its course. The community meetings occurred at larger intervals. In late February 1994, an exchange on the "lessons and callings from what we have experienced" shows the extent to which all things become "meaningful," such as the heading of a letter: "Field flowers do not move to another place to seek the sun's rays. God takes care of fertilizing them where they are." Thus, the brothers took root in Tibhirine. This is the place of grace—the same grace that accompanied the people of God and the disciples, as Brother Michel pointed out.

Three months later, the reasons for staying remained the same. The community dynamic grew in intensity and was marked by a certain wonder. Ties became closer. But this did not take away lucidity. "We've all had our fantasies, our moments of irrational fear, anticipation of a sure death!" Questions persisted but slowly a robust, renewed commitment took shape: prayer, conviviality, and then...: "LISTEN; RECONCILE mentally with the hardliners; EXPLAIN (the crisis, the fear, etc.); SHARE the danger, the crisis; HOPE. AN URGENCY: to continue to believe in this Algeria, this Islam, OTHERS, and to bear witness to it."

An exchange with the abbot general questioned their resolution. According to Dom Bernardo, "the Order needs monks more than martyrs." To which Brother Christian answered, "The two are not incompatible."

Accompanying one another amid turmoil required daily creativity. Other questions were raised by confronting the situation, especially how to deal with the information and the violence that was being communicated. By late April 1994, it

## Community Discernment amid Violence

became mandatory to take part in the community sharing. It was felt as a new means to strengthen one another mutually.

## MAY 1994 AND BEYOND: STEADFAST RESOLVE

In early May 1994, Sister Paul-Hélène and Brother Henri were assassinated in the monastery's library, leaving the community devastated. The library immediately reopened with another brother and sister, and life resumed. Two months later, we heard echoes of a renewed reflection on the reasons for staying: "to choose what the events impose on us."

The monks declined the apostolic nuncio's proposal to withdraw to Algiers, and at the end of the summer, the situation crystallized around two words: "Tenacious HOPE." But the assassinations of Sister Esther and Sister Caridad on October 23, 1994, sent the church into a state of shock. The monks carefully made sure to respect one another's freedom in the matter of staying or leaving. The bishops continued their work of consultation, encouragement, and preservation of a minimum ecclesial presence to prepare for the future.

During another community meeting on October 30, none of the brothers questioned the decision to stay, and no one saw himself anywhere else.

The anniversary of the Croatians' death was marked by the bishop's visit, who confirmed the community in its choices. He marveled at what he encountered: great communion among monks, unanimous resolve and mutual trust, closer relations with the neighbors, and self-abnegation.

In late December 1994, the church suffered another blow. Four White Fathers were assassinated in Tizi-Ouzou. The civil authorities offered protection—as they had done previously—but the monks declined once again.

## Witnesses of Synodality

## 1995: GRACE AND DIFFICULTY

With the arrival of spring 1995, eighteen months had passed since the "Christmas visit." Life had gone on, marked by a keen awareness of what it meant to be present in the name of the church at the service of the Algerians. The notes from the community meetings reveal a real grace, received in weakness and insecurity: a sense of widening and of deep listening, a new understanding of the sometimes difficult daily events. In his sharing, Brother Michel spoke about a covenant with the country: "In 1984 God granted me to marry the Algerian people as they were. The spouse has changed; with the brothers I feel called to continue, with all my misery. May He be blessed." Filled with gratitude, he mentioned once again the neighborhood as a source: "I have been helped a lot by the people around me (like Benali: I thank God that you are still alive)."

During the same sharing, brother Jean-Pierre noted the shift in the center of gravity toward "greater attention to the surroundings and to what the country is going through." He then formulated his interpretation of what was going on: "God wants something for us and through us. Because of this, no adversity can strike us: everything contributes to the accomplishment of that work."

Late 1995 brought another shock, directly affecting the church. On September 10, Sister Bibiane and Sister Angèle-Marie were fatally wounded while returning from Mass, and on November 10, Sister Odette was shot dead, her fellow sister surviving.

The Union of Major Superiors (USMDA) consulted the congregations that remained in Algeria with this theme: "our charism...in the current situation." The community sharing among the monks was rich. Because of the awareness that a charism "is not for oneself but for the good of others," they focused on the mission of ensuring a church presence, both contemplative and

Community Discernment amid Violence

attentive to the needs of those close to them. The reasons for staying were becoming stronger. Brother Paul saw this as a call to greater prayer and poverty. The prior insisted on the hope to live.

## 1996: OUTSIDE VISIT / THE DEATH OF SEVEN MONKS

In early January 1996, the theme of the next General Chapter of the Trappists was announced: "The Community as a School of Charity." In their sharing, the brothers marveled at the gift of community and at the contemplative outlook that had grown amid their predicaments. Thus, when Armand Veilleux, procurator of the order, visited the monks to evaluate their options, he encountered a mature community. The reason for coming over was also to carry out the regular "visit," a fraternal meeting usually held every two years by the abbot or abbess that, given the circumstances, had not taken place since the abbot general's visit in June 1991. The community felt that they needed this outside perspective. Dom Armand was impressed with what he saw and wrote to the brothers, "I believe that your community is spiritually and monastically at one of the best moments in its history."[5] The monks had managed to integrate into one community the variety of personal stories and each person's vocations, enjoying the grace of living the Trappist life together. In these dark hours, they were a community that was able to hold fast to the Cistercian charism in the simple life shared with their close neighbors, discerning from day to day, through individual meetings, community dialogue, and listening attentively in prayer, what was not compatible with it.

On the evening of March 26, 1996, the monks were gathered for the Ribât es Salâm meeting when seven of them were

---

5. "Carte de visite (January 19, 1996)," Moines de Tibhirine, *Heureux ceux qui espèrent: Autobiographies spirituelles* (Paris: Cerf, 2018), 46.

kidnapped by an armed group.[6] A few weeks later, they were assassinated.

## The Epiphany of a Synodal Community

So far, we have focused on how the monks grew in unity and clarity amid difficult circumstances, and on their ultimate death. In fact, the listening culture that we have encountered above was not new to the Monks of Tibhirine—in fact, it is central to the Rule of Saint Benedict. Indeed, in the annual circular letters sent to parents, friends, and relatives, we read examples of audacious decisions born from listening and discernment.

For example, in 1977, the monks donated two unoccupied rooms in the enclosure to the Little Sisters of Jesus, who were looking for a safe place to rest and pray. In 1988, they loaned a prayer room to villagers while their mosque was being built. That same year, they established a collaboration with four families to run the garden. And in 1990, when the "Bergerie de Berdine" asked for one of the monks to join them on a full-time basis, they proposed a twinning arrangement: one monk staying there for two months of the year and vice versa.[7] Convinced that their presence in Algeria was not only necessary but also wanted, the brothers never ceased to seek what human tenderness they could offer. They could not have reached this degree of relevance in the face of these events without constantly adjusting to one another in a spirit of mutual listening.

Moreover, mutual listening was part of the priorities of Brother Christian, the prior. A few days after his election, in his

---

6. The "Link of Peace" group was founded in 1979, and its mission was to gather the pearls of shared Muslim-Christian life experience.

7. The Bergerie de Berdine is a community in the south of France that takes in people caught up in alcohol or drug abuse or at odds with society.

## Community Discernment amid Violence

inaugural chapter,[8] he emphasized that the authority he had received was not a blank check but rather a gift to all. Calling everyone to coresponsibility in the sharing of tasks and talents, the new prior confessed his faith in the community, not without recalling that "there can only be community when there is an openness to contemplating the marvels of God hidden in each person."[9] In another homily held years earlier, he had preached that "every brother according to the flesh can become for me the Word of God."[10] According to Brother Christian, mutual listening and interpersonal relations made up and expressed the health of any community.

This kind of listening is a dynamic process that includes various elements. As we have observed above, events turned into occasions for listening to the thoughts, sentiments, and motives of the brothers and of others—both individually and as a community. It moved back and forth between the silence of prayer and sharing in community meetings. The intention was to listen to all thoughts, both fresh and ripe, so that, with the passing of time, their meaning for the community's common discernment would become clear.

The most consistent element in all this is the community's listening to scripture—the Word of God. For monks, this is obvious. Indeed, monastic life with its silence, common prayer, and personal prayer is organized around this. "Some of you have told me how much the Psalms speak to them now. We go to God's Word," noted Brother Christian. More than as a resource, the brothers considered being in touch with scripture as a necessary condition for embracing life and its demands. In a June 1994

---

8. A *chapter* is the monastic term for a meeting of the community.

9. Christian de Chergé, "Chapter (March 12, 1996)," in *Dieu pour tout jour: Chapitres de père Christian de Chergé à la communauté de Tibhirine, 1985–1996* (Godewaersvelde: Éd. de Bellefontaine, 2006), 549.

10. Christian de Chergé, "Homily 22nd Sunday in Ordinary Time (August 22, 1982)," in *L'Autre que nous attendons: Homélies de père Christian de Chergé, 1970–1996* (Godewaersvelde: Éd. de Bellefontaine, 2009), 74.

## Witnesses of Synodality

chapter, Christian recalled what Brother Henri Vergès—who was assassinated on May 8, 1994, along with Sister Paul-Hélène—had said about this to Brother Michel:

> What we expect from you are texts, words that have been meditated on (whether it be the Psalms, the readings or the prayer intentions in the Office, the introductions or the homilies at Mass). This also means that…if our words are to be alive and life-giving, they must be the fruit of our own experience, they must contain something of our own blood.[11]

Quoting what Brother Henri was hoping from the monks one month after he had been assassinated underlined the urgency of this essential imperative. It is by committing oneself to the Word of God that others will be able to have a taste of it. As Christian had said in an earlier chapter, in 1991:

> In his Word God has experienced the risk of entrusting himself to us.…We do not need to give him impetus…rather we have to let others find out that He is really our VITAL IMPETUS.[12]

## Conclusion

Thus, the Cistercian community of Tibhirine shows us how a synodal way of proceeding is possible even against the pressure of circumstances. The monks, in fact, deepened the discernment culture that they had inherited from their tradition and Rule. This culture is characterized by what one may call "wide-angle" or integral listening; it includes three dimensions.

---

11. Christian de Chergé, "Chapter (June 14, 1994)," in *Dieu pour tout jour*, 490–91.
12. Christian de Chergé, "Chapter (July 2, 1991)," in *Dieu pour tout jour*, 373.

## Community Discernment amid Violence

First, such integral listening has its source in a resolute acceptance of the Word of God (in *lectio divina*, liturgy, and prayer), in correlation with life as it unfolds. Second, integral listening creates space for authentic interpersonal relationships and mutual listening with all that this demands in terms of self-transcendence and conversion. Finally, it opens us to listening to life in general, with its variety of events and experiences, transforming this into understanding everything that happens in the light of God and his Providence. In this light, everything takes on meaning, everything becomes the Word, everything becomes gift.

Integral listening is crucial for any parish, community, or group. It is only through listening to scripture, to one another, and to events and circumstances placed at the heart of our personal and ecclesial life that we can embody the creativity of the Holy Spirit, here and now. It is only through holding together the past, the present, and the future in faith, hope, and charity that integral listening allows us to enter "the broad embrace of God."[13] Therefore, key words for every synodal process are "openness," "mutual interdependence," and "availability to the action of the Holy Spirit." This way of life calls on our will to bond together into one. It requires the faith that from the depths of even the most tragic events may emerge a life that is stronger than death.

Ultimately, it is this "instinctive awareness of a fraternity that is stronger than misfortune" (Brother Christian) and a readiness to be the loving face that our environment needs that makes the witness of the blessed monks of Tibhirine a beacon of light for the universal church today, in search of a new synodal fervor.

---

13. Pope Francis, "Address to the Faithful of the Diocese of Rome," September 18, 2021.

## Bibliography

de Chergé, Christian. *Dieu pour tout jour: Chapitres de père Christian de Chergé à la communauté de Tibhirine, 1985–1996.* Godewaersvelde: Éd. de Bellefontaine, 2006.

———. *L'Autre que nous attendons: Homélies de père Christian de Chergé, 1970–1996.* Godewaersvelde: Éd. de Bellefontaine, 2009.

———. *L'invincible espérance.* Paris: Bayard, 1997.

Francis, Pope. "Address to the Faithful of the Diocese of Rome." September 18, 2021.

Georgeon, Thomas. "Donner sa vie pour la gloire de T'aimer: Tibhirine ou un chemin communautaire vers le martyre." *Collectanea Cisterciensia* 68 (2006): 76–104.

Moines de Tibhirine. *Heureux ceux qui espèrent: Autobiographies spirituelles.* Paris: Ed. du Cerf, 2018.

# 7
# A Parish Experience of Synodality
## Holy Trinity Catholic Church, Georgetown

*Brian Flanagan**

If synodality is the path that "God expects of the Church of the third millennium," in the words of Pope Francis,[1] one challenge that Roman Catholics will face is gaining in the knowledge and skills of how to live synodally. At this moment, when the Catholic Church has entered into the multiyear Synod on Synodality, it is incumbent upon the church and its theologians to begin reporting upon the progress of the synod and carrying out some initial analysis on the strengths and weaknesses of this process. This chapter, therefore, begins the work of critical reflection upon the practice of synodality by focusing on the witness of one parish in its synodal experience.

---

1. Pope Francis, "Ceremony Commemorating the 50th Anniversary of the Institution of the Synod of Bishops," October 17, 2015, https://www.vatican.va/content/francesco/en/speeches/2015/october/documents/papa-francesco_20151017_50-anniversario-sinodo.html.

## Witnesses of Synodality

In addition to the analyses of the practice of synodality at the level of the universal church, it is also crucial to include the parish level. As the primary experience of church for many Catholics, parishes are a key location for the entire vision of synodality that Pope Francis is attempting to resurrect in the church. If synodality does not become part of our normal way of life at the parish level, then his call to become a synodal church will fail, or worse, will reduce synodality to a form of ecclesial superstructure or managerial strategy disconnected from the life of the church at its most local level.

This chapter, therefore, explores the specific synodal participation of my own parish, Holy Trinity Catholic Church, in the neighborhood of Georgetown in Washington, DC. Crucial aspects of our parish's long-standing forms of shared governance and decision-making, as well as some of the characteristics of our community, created the foundation for a robust and fruitful synodal process in ways that might be imitable in other parishes and synodal contexts. And, at the same time, through the course of our synodal consultations, we learned more about ourselves and about how we can go further along a synodal path together in the coming years.

We begin by describing the parish, including some of the long-standing practices that proved foundational for our synodal process. Second, we consider the ways in which the parish engaged in its consultations for the Synod on Synodality, as guided by our parish pastoral council and our pastor and ecclesial leadership. Finally, we highlight some concrete tools and suggestions for implementation of synodality at the parish level, and by extension at all of the levels of the church on our shared journey together.

## History and Characteristics

Holy Trinity Catholic Church was founded in 1787 and is the oldest Roman Catholic congregation in what is now Washington,

## A Parish Experience of Synodality

DC. From its origins, it was integrally connected to nearby Georgetown University and continues to be a ministry of the Society of Jesus. While there is much to be lauded in the parish's long history serving Catholics in Georgetown and beyond, in recent years, like Georgetown University, the parish has begun reckoning with the history of enslavement, segregation, and racism that marks its origins and almost all its history. Like Georgetown University, the leaders of the institution, including the founding pastor, Fr. Francis Neale, SJ, as well as numerous congregants, were deeply invested in the evils of slavery, and while enslaved and free Black Catholics likely constituted nearly a third of the congregation for much of its early history, that community remained segregated into the twentieth century.[2]

Holy Trinity exists in some tension with this history. On the one hand, the parish remains predominantly white, and the overall wealth of the parish reflects the length of its history as well as its location in Georgetown, today one of the more expensive neighborhoods in Washington, DC. At the same time, over the past sixty years Holy Trinity has become a center of postconciliar renewal, committed in its liturgy and its structures to forms of social justice advocacy and, especially in recent years, to unearthing and confronting its racial history. It remains a very large parish, comprising around five thousand households, with primary school from kindergarten through to the eighth grade, and up to six Masses each weekend. It is a parish of choice rather than a geographical parish for many if not most of its members, with more than twenty-five full- and part-time paid staff and many engaged volunteers.

Three current aspects of our parish as an institution are crucial foundations for the successes of our synodal process. First, the clergy of the Society of Jesus, including the current pastor, Fr. Kevin

---

2. Fuller descriptions of this history can be found on the parish's website: https://www.curavirtualis.com/blog/categories/history. See, especially, the excellent summary articles "Holy Trinity Parish and Race: An Overview," parts I and II, by parishioner Bernard A. Cook.

## Witnesses of Synodality

Gillespie, SJ, as well as the lay pastoral staff, are proactively collaborative in their leadership and ministry. If synodality involves modeling forms of shared discernment and dialogue that involve all the baptized, then the postconciliar leadership of Fr. Thomas Gavigan, SJ, and his commitment to lay empowerment ("the parish is the people") established a culture for his successors that envisioned the pastors and staff as coordinating and guiding their fellow Catholics in the parish rather than ruling over them.

A second foundational piece is connected—a long history of engaged, enthusiastic involvement on the part of lay members of the parish. The Parish Pastoral Council (PPC) established by Father Gavigan in the 1960s is a robust body that advises and assists the pastor in the leadership of the parish. As I will note again below, Father Gillespie was able to entrust the planning and execution of the synodal process to the PPC precisely because of its long-standing role in the parish.

Third, and finally, a key aspect of parish life that the synodal process was able to draw upon was prior experience in dialogical conversation, including around difficult and sensitive topics. In recent years, the parish already has held parish-wide listening sessions and dialogues on clerical sexual abuse; on the specific role of Theodore McCarrick, the former archbishop of Washington, in that abuse; on the status and experiences of LGBTQIA+ members of the parish; and on some of the racial history discussed above. Drawing upon traditions of Ignatian discernment and restorative justice circle methodology, members of the parish restorative justice team already had experience in leading parish-wide dialogues like those envisioned for the synodal process.

## The Synodal Process

The Synodal Process of the archdiocese of Washington began in October 2021 with an invitation to the parishes within

## A Parish Experience of Synodality

the archdiocese to host parish listening sessions in preparation for the archdiocesan listening sessions in March 2022. Based on our long history of lay leadership and collaboration, Father Gillespie entrusted the organization of the parish process to the PPC as the elected representatives of the parish, under the leadership of PPC president Tania Chomiak-Salvi and vice president Jennifer Dorsey. The planners originally envisioned a mix of in-person and online Zoom listening sessions, but given a surge in COVID-19 infections in January 2022, all but one of the listening sessions were conducted via Zoom. Six of these sessions were open to all registrants, but specific sessions were held for two groups. The first was for young adults in the parish, which was the only session that was able to be held in person before the pandemic restrictions increased. The second, and perhaps most innovative, was a special session for LGBTQIA+ Catholics that was intentionally extended widely in the greater Washington area to provide a forum both for parishioners and for LGBTQIA+ Catholics and former Catholics in the area to have their voices heard.

Each session focused upon three questions, streamlined for clarity, drawn from the archdiocesan synodal instructions, and featured small group/breakout conversations, followed by larger group reporting for wider listening. Members of the parish restorative justice team and others experienced in restorative circle processes, primarily from the parish's work on racial justice issues, functioned as "circle keepers" facilitating each group. Restorative circle methods focused on giving each member of the group equal opportunity to speak and be heard. Developed by practitioners working in legal and criminal contexts, restorative justice circle methods have been extended in recent years in classrooms, other educational contexts, and some ecclesial contexts.[3] In our parish, the presence of members formed in

---

3. For more on restorative justice circle process, see Kay Pranis, *The Little Book of Circle Processes: A New/Old Approach to Peacebuilding* (Intercourse, PA: Good Books,

these methods provided a concrete way of implementing the kind of "speaking with *parrhesia*/boldness" and "listening with humility" that are at the heart of synodal practice. Members of the circle speak in turn without interruption, with opportunities to respond in a regular, recurring pattern that allows for deep listening and response that avoids polarizing patterns of debate and argument. Additionally, the long-standing fostering of Ignatian forms of discernment through the parish's Ignatian spirituality offerings, including the use of the *Spiritual Exercises'* "Presupposition" of good intent in dialogue with others, shaped the spiritual culture within these sessions.[4] Parishioners were, in many cases, already experienced in prayerful discernment in dialogue as a way of responding to challenges and participating in ministries in the parish.

Over the course of eight weeks, between three and four hundred individuals participated in these sessions, or responded to a survey for those unable to attend a listening session. That is a relatively small percentage of the membership of the parish, but PPC president Chomiak-Salvi was happily surprised by how diverse a cross section of parishioners engaged in the process— while it drew many of the more engaged members of the parish, it was not simply an echo chamber of the "usual suspects," and the randomness of the open sessions provided opportunities for community members who might not have encountered each other regularly in such a large parish. "We were sitting in intimate discussions, face-to-face discussions, even if on Zoom,

---

2005). For more on the theory of restorative justice, see Howard Zehr, *The Little Book of Restorative Justice*, rev. ed. (Intercourse, PA: Good Books, 2015).

4. The Ignatian Presupposition was originally intended to allow for the director and retreatant doing the *Spiritual Exercises* to enter into conversation with a spirit of mutual charity and expectation of right intention, or at least nonheretical intention, in speaking. In recent years, many Jesuit institutions have used the Presupposition more broadly to create a culture of dialogue rooted in mutual expectation of good intentions. See the parish's particular understanding of the Ignatian Presupposition at https://trinity.org/ignatian-spirituality/ignatian-spirituality-resources/the-ignatian-presupposition/.

## A Parish Experience of Synodality

with people that we wouldn't run into at our Mass or in our ministry," she reported. Members of the PPC and of the pastoral staff also attended these sessions, and PPC members functioned as notetakers to capture the responses raised by participants.

From that data—responses to a survey, over twenty hours of synodal conversation, and nearly fifty pages of notes!—members of the PPC drafted both a twenty-one-page report for members of the parish and a four-page summary of their findings to fit the space constraints of the requested report to the archdiocese.[5] In both cases, the reports identified some major themes that recurred across the conversations, and privileged the direct voices of parishioners. The report identified five themes: (1) the strength of spirituality, especially engagement with Ignatian spirituality, at the parish level; (2) a call to maintain Holy Trinity's reputation as a welcoming place for LGBTQIA+ Catholics, with simultaneous frustration regarding the wider church's teaching on and treatment of LGBTQIA+ Catholics; (3) a consistent concern over the role of women in the church and the need for greater responsibility to be given to women in leadership, including the possibilities of diaconal or presbyteral ordination; (4) an appreciation of the active young adult community at Holy Trinity but a concern about the overall decline in the participation of young Catholics in the church; and (5) a strong emphasis on an understanding of the church as the entire people of God and not only the clergy or hierarchy, and opposition to forms of clericalism.

Deacon Charles Huber and others who attended multiple sessions noted how consistently the same issues were raised despite the differences between various groups. It was also noted how the very process of engaging with the parish allowed leaders to hear from parishioners in new ways. One thing that was surprising was "the *way* we learned it," Chomiak-Salvi said. They

---

5. This report is available at https://trinity.org/wp-content/uploads/2022/03/Results-of-the-Holy-Trinity-Parish-Synod-on-Synodality-Listening-Process.pdf.

might have learned things from the parish through a survey or anecdotes, "but sitting in a room of diverse people and having it come up spontaneously" was a new way of encountering the sense of the faithful of the parish. Another result was the contrast participants expressed between their experience of the Catholic Church in this particular parish and their fears over the wider trends or structures of the global Catholic Church. Appreciation of the parish's welcoming of LGBTQIA+ Catholics, for instance, or its empowerment of lay parishioners, were often tempered with awareness of how much of an outlier Holy Trinity may be. As Jennifer Dorsey, the vice president of the PPC, said, "I now have more insight into how our parish thinks about the complex duality of being both comfortable in our parish and dedicated to our faith but frustrated, disappointed, and angry with the church at the same time."

## Outcomes of the Synodal Process

The results from this process and the consequent reports were used in two ways. First, as requested, the shorter report was submitted to the archdiocese for its Synod Diocesan Synthesis Report, and delegates from the parish attended one of four diocesan listening sessions in spring 2022. In the Archdiocesan Synodal Synthesis Report, many of the issues raised in Holy Trinity were mentioned, though with different emphases and contextualized by the concerns raised by other parishes and institutions.[6] In happy contrast to some of the fears expressed by parishioners

---

6. Interestingly, and positively in my opinion, the need to be more welcoming of LGBTQIA+ Catholics is mentioned five times in the final document. And yet, at the same time, the concern expressed strongly at Holy Trinity to better value the leadership and dignity of women in the Church is neglected—"women" are mentioned only once. See Roman Catholic Archdiocese of Washington, *Diocesan Synthesis Report*, 2022, https://adw.org/about-us/resources/synod-archdiocesan-synthesis-report/.

## A Parish Experience of Synodality

that their voices would go nowhere, through this Diocesan Synthesis Report, as noted by Father Gillespie, "we were heard."

A second and perhaps more important outcome, however, is the way that the parish itself received the results of the synodal process and is continuing to build on it. This is crucial for engagement in synodality at the parochial level, if synodality is going to be seen as part of the regular life of the church and not simply the input of data for a process far removed from the real life of most Catholics. In addition to the final report, the pastor and the PPC have continued to work from what they learned through the synodal process. For example, in response to the sense of frustration in the parish over the roles of women in the church, particularly in our worship, Father Gillespie received permission from the archbishop for an experiment in lay reflections at select Sunday Masses; of the participants, all but one were women. Drawing upon the voices of the parish from the synod gave him additional leverage in asking the cardinal for permission to act creatively in responding to the parish's expressed desires.

In June 2023, the PPC updated the parish on the concrete measures that had been taken in the past year to respond to many of the topics raised during the listening sessions and outlined in the reports.[7] The pastor, PPC, and other leaders are now planning to have regular synodal listening sessions in the parish and to reach out more proactively to voices that might have been missed during the previous sessions. But all recognize that receiving and implementing synodality in the parish is just at its beginnings. As Father Gillespie said, the question he had for himself as a pastor at the end of this first process was, "Did I hear my people, and what are we going to do about what we heard?"

---

7. Available at https://trinity.org/wp-content/uploads/2023/06/Parish-Efforts-to-Address-Synod-Topics-of-Concern-within-Holy-Trinity.docx.pdf.

### Witnesses of Synodality

# Tools for Synodality at the Parish Level

What tools for synodality used in this parish experience might be useful to other parishes and to the wider church as it continues building on its synodal process? I can identify at least four.

## EMPOWERING AND TRUSTING LAY LEADERSHIP

A key aspect of the success of our parish's synodal process was the pastor's decision to empower our parish pastoral council to lead the synodal initiative, and the trust of their gifts that allowed this to happen collaboratively and smoothly. Lay leadership of the process gave it credibility, especially among parishioners initially suspicious of the synodal process, and modeled the valuing of all the baptized upon which Pope Francis's entire synodal vision is based. This delegation was not a form of clerical "absenteeism," for members of the clergy and professional pastoral staff were deeply involved throughout the process. Obviously, such trusting relationships are not built overnight, and our parish had the distinctive advantage of a long history of collaboration and lay co-responsibility in our parish. But, given the authority that the Catholic tradition gives to pastors as presiders, not only in liturgy but also in synodality, the willingness of pastors not only to allow lay involvement but also to actively empower lay leadership is crucial to synodality at the parish level. As Father Gillespie noted, it depended on him as a pastor fostering a sense of "we" and not just "me" at the level of leadership.

## DRAWING UPON THE DISTINCTIVE EXPERIENCES OF A PARISH

Holy Trinity's ability to draw upon members of its restorative justice ministry to devise and mediate the process for our

## A Parish Experience of Synodality

listening sessions provided a structure for the bold speaking and active listening that are crucial to synodality. Similarly, the parish's emphasis on Ignatian spirituality provided a shared spiritual context for these conversations to occur. It may be true that some of these practices—the restorative circle method of dialogue and engagement with the Ignatian presupposition of good intent, for example—might be useful for other parishes and institutions in their own synodal processes. But another lesson from Holy Trinity's synodal process is the strength of beginning with the tools that a parish has as a foundation for its distinctive form of synodal process. Another parish may have a very different spiritual identity. The long traditions of Benedictine discernment, or Franciscan values, and others described in the chapters of this book might be better starting points for that parish's synodal process than presuming a "one-size-fits-all" form of dialogue. The most vibrant ministries in a parish and their clerical and lay leadership will likely be resources for talent and experience in leading synodal conversations, even if this specific way of being church feels relatively new, as it is for many of us.

## CREATIVELY WELCOMING ALL

On one level, Holy Trinity's process was very successful in drawing in large numbers of engaged parishioners to share their experiences of the church. Online sessions allowed for a wide range of participation, even if the originally planned use of online and in-person modalities might have welcomed even more voices. Particularly impressive was our attempt to reach out to LGBTQIA+ Catholics as one of the ecclesial "peripheries" that our parish was especially well situated to welcome into dialogue. And yet, at the same time, there is much more work to be done in engaging more of the members of the congregation. Moving forward, synodality will require imaginative ways to make the synodal encounter possible for all members

## Witnesses of Synodality

of the parish. At Trinity, for example, future synodal conversations need to think through how to reach out to working parents and gig-economy workers with limited time for long conversations; to parishioners with less access to online possibilities; to more alienated Catholics, including but extending beyond the LGBTQIA+ members, who no longer feel part of the community; and to the large number of parishioners who are registered in the parish or school but for other reasons did not engage in the synodal process. If synodality is not to become an echo chamber of the "usual suspects" of a parish who already think the same way, leadership teams must continue to experiment with new ways of inviting the entire community into the synodal conversation.

## IMAGINING THE FUTURE

This leads to a final crucial "tool" for implementing synodality at the parish level—the collective imagination, of both the leadership and congregation—of what a synodal church looks like in the future. Leaders at Holy Trinity have already shared what they learned in their first synodal process and are beginning to imagine what regular synodal dialogue at the parish can mean. Like Pope Francis, they recognize that synodality cannot be a one-off attempt but must be part of the "normal order" of a functioning church, a way of being church rather than a momentary interruption. Continuing to engage synodally at the parish level, even after the current Synod on Synodality has ended or without directives or initiatives from above, is the only way in which the fragile replanting of synodality in the life of the church that we are currently witnessing can be nourished, be sustained, and grow into the future that our God wants for us.

## Bibliography

Francis, Pope. "Ceremony Commemorating the 50th Anniversary of the Institution of the Synod of Bishops." October 17, 2015. https://www.vatican.va/content/francesco/en/speeches/2015/october/documents/papa-francesco_20151017_50-anniversario-sinodo.html.

Holy Trinity Catholic Church. *Results of the Holy Trinity Parish Synod on Synodality Listening Process*. March 16, 2022. https://trinity.org/wp-content/uploads/2022/03/Results-of-the-Holy-Trinity-Parish-Synod-on-Synodality-Listening-Process.pdf.

Pranis, Kay. *The Little Book of Circle Processes: A New/Old Approach to Peacebuilding*. Intercourse, PA: Good Books, 2005.

Roman Catholic Archdiocese of Washington. *Diocesan Synthesis Report*. 2022. https://adw.org/about-us/resources/synod-archdiocesan-synthesis-report/.

Zehr, Howard. *The Little Book of Restorative Justice*. Rev. ed. Intercourse, PA: Good Books, 2015.

\* I am deeply grateful for the conversations with Fr. Kevin Gillespie, SJ, the pastor of Holy Trinity; Tania Chomiak-Salvi and Jennifer Dorsey, the president and vice president, respectively, of the parish pastoral council; and Deacon Charles Huber, and to all the members of the parish in the preparation of this chapter.

# 8

# A Diocesan Experience of Synodality

## San Diego

*John E. Hurley, CSP*

Shortly after the election of Pope Francis, Archbishop Emeritus John Raphael Quinn of San Francisco was in Rome. He had the distinct pleasure of concelebrating Mass with the new pope in his residence. In his homily, Pope Francis said that "synodality is the path of the Catholic Church." Archbishop Quinn was ecstatic at hearing these words. As he was leaving the chapel, the holy father told him "that he had read [his] recent book on structures of communion and without commenting on the book itself he mentioned how 'important' the subject of collegiality and synodality are for the Church today."[1]

---

1. This was shared in an interview shortly afterward with Vatican correspondent Gerard O'Connell; see Gerard O'Connell, "Impressed by Pope's Emphasis on Synodality in the Church," *La Stampa* (July 22, 2013), https://www.lastampa.it/vatican-insider/en/2013/07/22/news/impressed-by-pope-s-emphasis-on-synodality-in-the-church-1.36075693/.

# A Diocesan Experience of Synodality

I know Archbishop Quinn from the time I served under him as pastor of Old St. Mary's Cathedral. During that time, I worked closely and began a long friendship with Father Robert McElroy, now Cardinal McElroy and the bishop of San Diego. I had a unique experience working with him on two diocesan synods in 2016 and 2019. Moreover, I have served as a consultant to the diocesan synod commission overseeing its response for the Synod 2021–2024. In this chapter, I share how this pioneering synodal journey unfolded, as well as insights from it, with the hope that it will inform and inspire others who are open to the Holy Spirit and committed to authentic synodality.

## Diocesan Synod 2016: Embracing the Joy of Love

### BACKGROUND

In early 2016, Cardinal McElroy shared with me that he wanted a diocesan synod on the expected apostolic exhortation following the 2015 Synod of Bishops on "The Vocation and Mission of the Family in the Church and Contemporary World." When the document was released, the cardinal invited me to coordinate the diocesan response. Thus began an adventurous journey together. I remember one of our early conversations, when he shared, "I have no idea where this synod process is going and what they will come up with." I responded, "It's tough to trust in the Holy Spirit, so let's go for the ride." Indeed, trusting in the Holy Spirit is key to a successful synodal process.

Such a process was opportune for the diocese due to the retirement of the codirectors of the Marriage and Family Life Office. At the time, the office was engaged mostly, although not exclusively, in marriage preparation sessions. Clearly, the signs of the times were saying that, for generations today, family life is

## Witnesses of Synodality

more complex. Maybe something in addition to marriage preparation was needed? The cardinal wanted to consider what a new office could focus on, in light of the apostolic exhortation *Amoris Laetitia* (The joy of love) that was released in 2016, shortly after our initial conversation about the synod.

## EXPERIENCE

Following the release of the apostolic exhortation, the cardinal invited key pastoral leaders to discern areas of focus in preparation for a diocesan synod. After a few sessions, it was decided that the cardinal would write a pastoral letter sharing five challenges for the synodal process to discern:

1. the challenge to witness to both the beauty and the reality of the Catholic vision of marriage and family life,
2. the challenge to form a culture of invitation and hospitality to unmarried couples,
3. the challenge to welcome, nurture, and form children,
4. the challenge to provide authentic pastoral support for those who are divorced, and
5. the challenge to bring spiritual depth to family life.

Importantly, it was also decided that the diocesan synod would be the most significant level of dialogue, discernment, and decision-making in the life of the diocese. In a deep spiritual orientation to the wider life of the diocese, the synod would include theological reflection, pastoral insight, and visioning and governance implications.

All one hundred parish pastors of the diocese were asked to nominate a delegate to represent their parish. Various family-oriented ministries were invited to nominate delegates as well. The deans and members of the priests' council would also be

## A Diocesan Experience of Synodality

delegates. Finally, the cardinal appointed ten at-large members and six theologians to be engaged in various aspects of the process. This was a true test for the relatively new San Diego bishop in his openness to the Holy Spirit since he was still getting to know the priests. Later, we realized that the Holy Spirit was truly a part of the nomination process.

Delegates were offered a first and second choice of the challenge working group of which they wished to be a member. Over the course of the summer, the delegates invited their parishioners to gather and seek input regarding their respective challenges, so that they would bring more than their own perspective to the working group meetings. One Saturday was devoted to each of the topics with the delegates and theologians present. Each working group was divided into smaller groups and focused on each of the questions from the pastoral letter. Proposals were considered and prioritized for presentation at the synod general assembly. At the end of each of five Saturday working groups, the cardinal joined in, and the proposals were shared with him.

The general assembly consisted of 125 delegates evenly divided between men and women with ethnic and generational diversity. Each of the five challenge working groups consisted of 25 delegates. Diocesan staff served as facilitators and took minutes. The working groups presented a total of forty-six proposals to the assembly that were narrowed down to fifteen—three for each of the challenges. The Synod Implementation Committee was now formed and consisted of various leaders with shared expertise in the focus areas addressed throughout the synodal process.

## TODAY

The Synod Implementation Committee recommended a change of name for the Marriage and Family Life Office to the Office for Family Life and Spirituality. A new director, who could embrace the proposals of the synod process, was sought. Now

### Witnesses of Synodality

in its seventh year, the committee, which consists of four core members and a few collaborators, focuses on eight areas, which are: marriage formation, family spirituality, marriage enrichment, Celebrating Your Love diocesan retreats, separated and divorced ministry, fertility awareness, healing pathways for families, and mental health ministry. Some parishes have Family Life Committees that are starting to minister to groups such as the widowed, separated, and divorced, and to the LBGTQ+ community. About one-third of the parishes have implemented a new marriage preparation program, *Witness to Love*, that includes mentoring couples on dialoguing about their relationship in a way that integrates modern psychology. In 2021, when we celebrated the fifth anniversary of the synod, it was amazing to see so many people gather from all walks of family life.

# Diocesan Synod 2019: Christ Lives! A Time of Dreams and Decisions

## BACKGROUND

In 2019, following the 2018 Synod of Bishops on "Young People, Faith and Vocational Discernment," the cardinal invited me to coordinate a second diocesan synod.[2] This diocesan synod was unique in that it was not *about* young adults but convened *with* young adults. We wanted to hear about their dreams for the church.

## EXPERIENCE

Like the previous diocesan synod in 2016, the cardinal invited key pastoral leaders to discern how the apostolic exhorta-

---

2. The Post-Synodal Apostolic Exhortation *Christus Vivit* (Christ is alive) was issued in 2019.

## A Diocesan Experience of Synodality

tion was challenging us. After a few sessions, it was determined that this diocesan synod would provide a time for young adults to dream big and to make decisions about walking with Christ in such a way that the local church would accompany them. The following five objectives of the synod emerged:

1. *Walking with God*: young adults will evaluate their spiritual and personal relationship with God.
2. *Walking with the Church*: young adults will assess their perception of the Catholic Church today.
3. *Walking in Solidarity*: young adults will explore how they are welcomed and accompanied in their parish communities.
4. *Walking with a Purpose*: young adults will explore their calling and purpose in life by assessing their leadership, their sense of social service, and the difference they make as a Christian.
5. *Walking toward Freedom*: as people freed by Christ, young adults will explore how the diocese and/or parishes can support them in living out this freedom for fullness of life and mission.

Participants in this synod would include both single young adults and young adult couples between the ages of eighteen and thirteen. Each parish would be represented by one single young adult or one young adult couple. The diocesan seminarians would also participate, along with the deans and members of the Priests' Council. There were a total of 133 delegates, with an average age of twenty-nine (clergy included). The delegates were equally divided between men and women with a richness of ethnic and generational diversity.

At the assembly, we watched a video with a series of interviews with students from the campus of San Diego State University. In the interviews, students shared their views of the Catholic

## Witnesses of Synodality

Church. Many of them identified as Catholic yet nonpracticing, and some were active in parish life. In general, they appreciated being invited to share their thoughts and experiences.

The synod process comprised two parts. The first part consisted of seven deanery gatherings; the second part was the General Assembly. By working with the deaneries, we were acknowledging that young adults tend to float among parishes that have young adult activities. The parish delegates invited single young adults and young adult couples (dating, engaged, or married) to participate in a deanery session to reflect on each of the five topics mentioned above. Tables discussed different "walking with" themes and developed proposals, with everyone prioritizing their choice under each topic.

The Synod Core Team reviewed all seventy-nine proposals from the seven deaneries. Recognizing that topics overlapped and that others could be merged, the team reduced the number of proposals to thirty-two, which were then discussed by the General Assembly for further discernment and for taking decisions and implementing. The General Assembly delegates were divided into five working groups, with each focusing on one of the "walking with" topics.

At the end of the General Assembly, each group contributed five proposals for each of the five "walking with" themes, of which the top two would be implemented immediately. The cardinal added two proposals. The first was that by the end of 2022, each parish would have 25 percent of its liturgical and leadership roles filled with young adults. The second was that by January 2020, a Deanery Young Adult Leadership Team would meet with the two delegates from each parish, and a Diocesan Young Adult Commission would be formed and include two representatives from each deanery.

The cardinal and I had discussed these two proposals beforehand. We wanted this energized group of leaders to go home with some concrete ideas to share with their deaneries.

## A Diocesan Experience of Synodality

Prior to the General Assembly, the director of schools and the synod coordinator convened a gathering of young adult teachers and administrators from Catholic schools. This gathering developed five proposals exclusively for the school community, which were presented to the General Assembly. Cardinal McElroy approved all the proposals on November 9, 2019, at the Mission of San Diego de Alcalá.

One key outcome from this synod was the realization that there needs to be two tracks for young adult ministry: one for single young adults (post-high school, workers, college students, and professional workers), and one for coupled young adults (dating, engaged, newly married, and those with and without children). Moreover, singles should no longer be seen as dependent. As one single young adult reported at one of the listening sessions, "Pastoral leadership needs to stop looking at single young adults as dependents. I am a corporate real estate agent, and I have financial capacity and a lot to offer a parish." At all the listening sessions, I was usually the oldest in the room, and I must say that this synod process gave me much hope for the church.

## TODAY

The implementation of the synod proposals was slowed down due to the pandemic. Today, the Young Adult Office is staffed by three people who are working to further implement the proposals. A new director took over not long after the synod; the fact that he had participated in the synod process was a blessing. The deaneries' young adult committees and the diocesan young adult commission are moving forward. The results of the universal synod report for the United States and the diocese gives additional impetus to young adult ministry and higher priority to the diocesan synod proposals.

Witnesses of Synodality

# The Diocesan Phase of the 2021–2024 Synod

## BACKGROUND

The two diocesan synods have clearly fostered greater communion and participation in the Diocese of San Diego, as well as a greater interest and engagement in mission. For this synodal process, my role shifted from coordinator to consultant; it is run by the Diocesan Synod Commission. Its members are committed to one another and to the synodal process. They are excited about the renewed sense of mission and approach.

## 2022 EXPERIENCE

At the beginning of the process, the Diocesan Synod Commission formed a steering committee to oversee the day-to-day aspects of facilitating a true synodal process. The co-chairs were Maria Olivia Galvan, the chancellor and director of Pastoral Ministries, and Robert Ehnow, the director of the Life, Peace, and Justice Office. One major agenda item was to ask the pastors to appoint a parish synod coordinator. These coordinators are heroes to the parish process. This committee took care of the framework for the parish and nonparochial participation, formulated questions for reflection, contacted media to engage greater participation across many spectrums, and facilitated the compilation and review of all input and data. It also engaged the expertise and guidance of researchers from the University of San Diego. All aspects of the process were presented to the Diocesan Synod Commission for their input and approval.

Subsequently, parishes held listening sessions. They were held in the evenings, during the day, or on the weekends, depending on the local demographics. These listening sessions used a specific method, the so-called council process for small groups

## A Diocesan Experience of Synodality

that has Native American roots. Decision-makers would sit in a circle and only speak when a symbol was passed to them.[3] In our case, the facilitator would pass a small cross to someone in the small group enabling them to speak, and then the cross would be passed to another. This also allowed for more gracious listening to one another rather than immediately thinking of what you would say. This worked very well given the polarization currently present in society and the church. Each small group had a facilitator and a secretary who took minutes.

Participants were invited to share their reflections on the following:

> Tell us about a time when you experienced disappointment with the church.
> Tell us about a time when you experienced joy with the church.
> As you leave this experience, express a hope you have for the church.

Overall, there were some eleven hundred sessions held across parishes, schools, religious groups, and prisons, and over eleven thousand people participated. The overwhelming initial response when sessions concluded was that people wanted more of this kind of conversation. As one person expressed, "I have never been asked for my thoughts about my experience in the church by anyone…this is great!"

Reports were sent to the diocesan office collating the information for the diocese. Our researchers assisted the cardinal and committee in preparing the report for the United States Conference of Catholic Bishops (USCCB).

However, this was not the end for the diocese. The diocesan report served as a framework for an anonymous diocesan-wide

---

3. The OJAI Foundation also adapted this model of "council" for small group discussion in circles.

## Witnesses of Synodality

survey that would hopefully reach a wider audience through the internet and parish electronic means. Over twenty-seven thousand survey responses were received and collated by our researchers from the University of San Diego. This information can then be broken down further to offer insights for the future direction of mission in the diocese.

## 2023 EXPERIENCE

At the time of writing this chapter, we are looking forward to another synodal gathering, focused on "Building Eucharistic Communities." Realizing that the bishops in the United States are calling Catholics across the country to a "Eucharistic Revival" through 2024, the cardinal wanted to continue the diocesan consultation process complimenting the bishops' focus on real presence. These consultation sessions took place in October 2023.

The conversations will consider the following:

> Tell us about a meaningful experience you or someone close to you had when participating in the Eucharist.
> Tell us about a challenge you or someone close to you experienced related to the Eucharist.
> As you leave this experience, how can you be the living presence of Jesus in your parish and community?

## Conclusion

For the last eight years, under the leadership of Cardinal McElroy, the diocese of San Diego has grown in its commitment to synodality. The Apostle Paul offers a beautiful image for this path by describing the church as a body: "Now you are the body

## A Diocesan Experience of Synodality

of Christ and individually members of it" (1 Cor 12:27). How do we progress on this path of co-responsibility? Rather than sketching procedures and detailing processes, let me conclude by recommending some crucial virtues that our experience in San Diego taught us.

One cannot walk this path unless there is authentic openness to the Holy Spirit. As Dr. Carolyn Woo shared in a panel response at the 2022 Leadership Roundtable Summit, "I often used to ask the Holy Spirit to guide me in what I am doing; and then I realized I had it backward."

Clergy cannot walk this path alone. Co-responsibility is a consequence of the dignity of baptism. Where would we be in the church without women and the resources of the laity in general?

Gracious listening is essential. It is necessary to have the capacity to listen carefully to every word a person is saying rather than formulating a response while they are still speaking. As a Paulist father once said in a homily when I was a seminarian, "You can listen people into existence."

Accompaniment along the path is key before we even begin to speak to someone else. Are we truly willing to understand, appreciate, and sometimes empathize with someone whose experience is different from my own rather than making a judgment?

The richness of diversity in our parishes is a blessing along the path of synodality. My way is not always the only way. We are all members of the Body of Christ, yet we have different spiritualities, different cultures, different backgrounds, different generations and experiences of our church and society. The complexities in our family life today can turn challenges into blessings in our families, in our church, and in our society.

New pastors and leaders in ministry can use a synodal process along their path as they chart out future directions. Pastoral

## Witnesses of Synodality

leaders are called to lead by embracing the above as gifts in the process.

We have listened along the path; now comes the time for the church to consult with the Body of Christ along the path of synodality.

# 9

# Australia's Plenary Council

## Richard Lennan

During the two sessions (October 2021 and July 2022) of their Plenary Council, Australian Catholics became familiar with references to the event as the "Fifth Plenary Council of Australia." This numbering could convey the impression that such councils were a well-established feature of Australian ecclesial practice. The reality is otherwise. In fact, the Fourth Plenary took place in 1937, leaving some eighty-five years before it had a successor. Since the world and church of 1937 differed dramatically from all that prevails in the twenty-first century, the plenary of 2021–22 carved out a new path for Australian Catholics. While a response to the church's present-day circumstances, the plenary sought also to be a faithful reception of the living tradition, and to further the discipleship and mission of Australian Catholics beyond 2022.

Path making is rarely a neat or simple exercise. As they contend with unexpected obstacles along the way, those forging a path must resist two contradictory temptations: to disdain the possible and useful in favor of an unattainable perfection or to neglect vision and effort in favor of illusory easy solutions.

## Witnesses of Synodality

Negotiating these challenges calls for creativity and patience, as well as generous openness to sources of wisdom other than one's own. Without these positive qualities, barriers to path making become insurmountable, and those making the path divide into factions that scorn shared striving. Since Australia's plenary neither disintegrated into partisanship nor defaulted to "quick fixes," it can be a beacon for other communities engaging synodal processes.

To support its claim that the plenary was a path-making event, this chapter will first summarize the preparation for the 2021–22 assemblies, concentrating on the key features of the plenary's commitments and methodology. Next, the chapter will consider aspects of the plenary's two assemblies to bring into relief the link between methodology and outcomes while also showcasing the creativity required of participants when they encountered unanticipated complications. The final section of the chapter will identify lessons from Australia's plenary applicable to the co-responsible discernment of other local churches as they construct paths for their pilgrimage to the fullness of God's reign.

## The Preparatory Phase

The instrument that guided every stage of the plenary's work was the commitment to listen to what the Holy Spirit might be saying to the church in Australia.[1] This commitment echoed the summons to the first Christian communities (cf. Rev 2:7, 11, 17, 29; 3:6, 13, 22). More proximately, the commitment to listen to the Spirit for the sake of renewed discipleship resonates strongly with Pope Francis's understanding of synodality.

---

1. The website for the Plenary Council—https://plenarycouncil.catholic.org.au/—provides a comprehensive record of the history and documents for every step of the plenary process, beginning with the consultation phase in 2018 through to the 2022 assembly in Sydney.

As is well-known, Francis describes synodality in the life of the church as a process of "mutual listening in which everyone has something to learn. The faithful people, the college of bishops, the Bishop of Rome: all listening to each other, and all listening to the Holy Spirit, the 'Spirit of truth' (Jn 14:17), in order to know what 'the Spirit says to the Churches' (Rev 2:7)."[2]

The focus on the Spirit brings to the fore both the church's sacramental nature and its orientation toward fulfillment in Jesus Christ. As sacrament, the church is the product of grace and human freedom that either illuminates or obscures the Spirit's grace. Grace is an enduring stimulus to the church's conversion, so listening to the Spirit's wisdom and guidance fosters the authenticity of the Christian community's mission and worship.

The emphasis on the Spirit distinguishes synodality from a parliamentary or administrative process, without reducing it to a spiritual exercise devoid of "real-world" implications. If the measure of authentic listening is the willingness to move in response to what is heard, then openhearted attention to the Spirit, far from being a retreat from the messy reality of everyday life, can be an instrument for reform of the church.[3] Grace fosters change in the church by inspiring the quest to ensure that the Christian community's pastoral priorities, liturgical practices, and forms of governance are evermore faithful to the gospel.

A grace-centered ecclesiology has as its corollary the importance of hearing the voices of all the baptized. This is so as every member of the church receives the Spirit's gifts and shares in the universal priesthood of the baptized. The recognition that

---

2. Pope Francis, "Ceremony Commemorating the 50th Anniversary of the Institution of the Synod of Bishops"; https://www.vatican.va/content/francesco/en/speeches/2015/october/documents/papa-francesco_20151017_50-anniversario-sinodo.html.

3. For the link between listening to the Spirit and moving, see Eboni Marshall Turman, "The Holy Spirit and the Black Church Tradition: Womanist Considerations," in *The Holy Spirit and the Church: Ecumenical Reflections with a Pastoral Perspective*, ed. Thomas Hughson (New York: Routledge, 2016), 111.

## Witnesses of Synodality

grace suffuses the community of faith is crucial for the practice of synodality.

To do justice to the omnipresence of the Spirit, the process of listening that guided the Plenary Council was open to all people who chose to speak, irrespective of their relationship to the church. Soon after the Australian Catholic Bishops Conference decided in 2018 to hold the plenary, listening sessions began around the country. These sessions 220,000 people across Australia and prompted 70,000 written and electronic submissions. Through these mechanisms, Australian Catholics, and many people who were not members of the church, expressed their convictions, desires, and laments about the church. As they did so, there was no censoring of opinions or imposition of limits on what qualified as acceptable topics.

After the listening sessions, organizers of the plenary were responsible for sifting through all the feedback received. This sifting sought to identify the key themes that would become the raw material for the plenary's discernment. A steering committee that included bishops, theologians, and representatives of those who would be participants in the plenary then produced a working paper that became the basis for reflection at the first assembly of the plenary in October 2021.

Before examining the 2021 session, it is important to acknowledge that both the distillation of the material gleaned from the listening sessions and the development of the working papers were subject to critique for a lack of transparency. In this context, an oft heard accusation against the two processes was that they were insufficiently inclusive of topics, such as gender and sexuality, that emerged during the nationwide listening phase.

Irrespective of whether the accusation was justified, the critique highlights an inherent limitation of the synodal process: that it is necessarily selective, choosing some themes while overlooking others. Synodality can provide opportunities for every voice to be heard, but the transition from opinion gathering to discernment and decision-making requires choices about what issues to carry forward. Making these choices is rarely easy. It is especially fraught in the present era when institutions and authorities are regularly subject to the hermeneutic of suspicion and social media amplifies every expression of discontent and distrust.

While suspicion might be ineradicable, the history of the Second Vatican Council offers a narrative with the potential to mollify its excesses. The council's history, especially the bishops' rejection of the original version of the documents, underscores that a synodal gathering need not be a "rubber stamp" for the first draft of texts. Transparency in the production of documents is certainly crucial, but it is the reception of the texts by participants in the synod process that is the ultimate arbiter of their value. If the synodal assemblies prize free exchange among participants, and the openness to the Spirit that such exchanges embody, it is likely that the gatherings will move in directions that no preparatory drafts can dictate. The next two sections of this chapter will explore the plenary's assemblies with a focus on such movement.

## The Assembly of October 2021

The gathering in Sydney in July 2022 is likely to be what will define "the Plenary Council" for future generations of Australian Catholics. There are good reasons for this assessment, but a full portrait of the plenary requires engagement with the assembly of October 2021. A review of the first assembly, therefore, can contribute to an appreciation of what the Australian experience might offer to the wider church.

In the initial design for the plenary, the first assembly was to be held in Adelaide. As the capital of South Australia, the state that sits between the east coast, where three cities (Brisbane,

## Witnesses of Synodality

Sydney, and Melbourne) together account for half of the total number of Australians, and the geographically vast but more sparsely populated west coast, Adelaide offered a theoretical "midpoint" for a national gathering. South Australia is also the state with a particular association with Saint Mary of the Cross MacKillop, Australia's only canonized saint, who was at the heart of the national prayer campaign in preparation for the plenary. Ultimately, the assembly did not meet in Adelaide: in the wake of the COVID-19 pandemic, with its lockdowns and travel restrictions, the assembly was held entirely online.

The shift to an online gathering generates two insights relevant to synodality. First, it serves as a reminder that all events in the life of the church take place in history. History, the flow of time, is unpredictable: it might even include a once-in-a-century global pandemic. This fact might seem too obvious to merit mention, but it reinforces that effective synodality must be aware of and responsive to the world as it is, not as it once was or as people of faith might wish it to be. Effective synodality, then, affirms that the Christian community is not a timeless body insulated from the world's concerns. For Australia's plenary, COVID-19 strikingly communicated this truth.

Reinforcing the church's grounding in history, the second salient point about the assembly's switch from in-person to online mode concerns the use of modern technology. For a week, the online assembly brought together, across multiple time zones, more than two hundred members of the plenary, plus all the associated theologians and support staff, and as many "everyday" people who wanted to watch the daily public sessions of the proceedings. Not too many years earlier, the pandemic would have resulted in the cancellation of the assembly. In 2021, however, Microsoft Teams and a cohort of skilled technicians enabled the assembly to proceed seamlessly. The use of an online platform would not yet be an option for a synodal gathering in many parts of the world, but there are few places still untouched by technology. What burgeoning technology might mean for the life of the church, including for synodality, is an open question, but one demanding attention.[4]

Beyond logistical issues, reflection on the methodology of the first assembly can enhance an appreciation of the dynamics of synodality. Here, the key point is that the first assembly was not a decision-making forum. As the plan for the plenary was always that there would be two assemblies, the online week was a period of discernment related to all that emerged from the earlier listening sessions. The specific purpose of the first assembly was to identify themes and topics that could crystallize the agenda for the gathering in 2022. The online assembly introduced the plenary's core mechanism for this discernment: "spiritual conversations," which began with a reading from scripture. James McEvoy captures well the dynamics of these conversations:

> The reading of the scriptural passage was followed by five minutes of silent meditation, then three rounds of members' contributions. First, without comment from other members, each one shared what they had heard in their own prayer and how that left them feeling. Second, and again without comment, members shared what they had discerned the Spirit saying through the voices of the group and how that left them feeling. Third, an open conversation ensued about the import of the group's sharing for the motions under consideration.[5]

Thus, these spiritual conversations established the plenary as a discernment process rather than one focused on debates

---

4. See, for example, Agnes M. Brazal, "Synodality and the New Media," *Theological Studies* 84, no. 1 (2023): 95–109, and John Roberto, ed. *Digital Ministry and Leadership in Today's Church* (Collegeville, MN: Liturgical Press, 2022).

5. James Gerard McEvoy, "Pope Francis on the Practice of Synodality and the Fifth Australian Plenary Council," *Theological Studies* 84, no. 1 (2023): 89.

and votes. The conversations demonstrated that attentiveness to God's word and the grace of shared wisdom could be catalysts for questions and critical reflections on the church's practices and policies while simultaneously challenging all participants to conversion.

In this way, the first assembly conveyed to the whole Catholic community that "the church" could differ from a top-down institution, an unstructured collective, or a fragile coalition of fractious partisans. The assembly made present an experience of the church as a community of the baptized. Within this community, members have specific roles and responsibilities, but the shared gift of the Holy Spirit transcends all differences. Accordingly, the spiritual conversation groups brought together members of the plenary across a range of demographic factors, social status, and ecclesial roles.[6] Remarkably, all of this took place within a "virtual" gathering.

# The Assembly of July 2022

The period between the two assemblies was a time of intense activity for the steering committee responsible for producing the document that would be the working text for the second assembly. From the many hundreds of reflections that emerged from the first assembly, the steering committee chose the eight themes on which the plenary would vote. Various writing groups, composed of the plenary's theological advisors—the *periti*—and other contributors, then elaborated on those themes for the continuing formation of members of the plenary. The steering committee finalized the draft motions, which were distributed to members well in advance of the gathering in Sydney.

---

6. For a series of reflection on the first assembly, see Richard Lennan, Ormond Rush, Gerard Kelly, and James McEvoy, "Theological Reflections on the First Assembly of the Plenary Council," *Australasian Catholic Record* 99, no. 2 (2022): 131–45.

## Australia's Plenary Council

Despite concerns about the continuing impact of the pandemic, the second assembly convened as scheduled in Sydney on July 3, beginning with a Sunday evening liturgy at the grave of Mary MacKillop. On the Monday morning, the voting members of the plenary, theological advisors, ecumenical observers, and a host of people responsible for the assembly's logistics all met face-to-face. While the online gathering for the first assembly was certainly effective in facilitating the plenary's discernment, the symbolic power of the assembly hall filled with people representative not only of all Australian states and territories but also of the range of Catholic rites—including Maronites, Syro-Malabar, and Melkites—present in Australia was incomparable as an expression of "the church."

There are, of course, myriad aspects of the second assembly that merit comment and discussion. This section, however, will limit itself to two topics: the "contextual" nature of the motions discussed and accepted, and the process that the assembly employed when it experienced its most contentious issue. Both topics demonstrate the path-making quality of the plenary.

Since the Second Vatican Council, "the local church," whether as a diocese or even a whole nation, has become a staple of Catholic ecclesiology and pastoral life. The emphasis on the particularity of each local church mitigates an earlier sense that the Catholic Church was always and everywhere "the same." The plenary strongly endorsed the need for the Australian Catholic community to engage in mission in ways attuned to its context. This endorsement is evident in the first two sets of motions that the Sydney assembly accepted: one set addressed "Reconciliation: Healing Wounds, Receiving Gifts" in the church's relationship with Australia's Aboriginal and Torres Strait Islander people; the second committed the Catholic community to "Choosing Repentance—Seeking Healing" in the wake of the sexual abuse crisis, which was the initial catalyst for the plenary as a whole.

## Witnesses of Synodality

By prioritizing these themes, the Plenary affirmed its identity as an activity of the Catholic Church in Australia.

The most memorable event of what was an extraordinary week in Sydney came on the assembly's third day, when the required two-thirds of episcopal voters failed to endorse the motions on "Witnessing to the Equal Dignity of Women and Men." These motions, which sought to expand opportunities for women's participation in ecclesial ministry and leadership, were of the utmost importance for many members of the assembly, and of the wider Catholic community. The rejection of the motions could have derailed the whole plenary, dividing members into warring camps defined by their perception of episcopal authority. That this worst-case scenario was not the outcome testifies to a consistent application of the plenary's core principle: listening to the Holy Spirit.

In the context of the failed motions, "listening" involved acknowledging that the tension resulting from the vote made it impossible to proceed with the assembly's scheduled agenda. Instead of pressing forward, the assembly set up an ad hoc committee to rework the failed motions, not to diminish them but to clarify and strengthen them. After further discernment, the bishops and the full assembly were able to achieve a near-unanimous endorsement of the revised motions. This result was not the triumph of politics and lobbying but of the commitment to hear the Spirit at work in the whole assembly. The initial rejection of the motions cast a shadow over the assembly but, paradoxically, became the vehicle for a ringing endorsement of what synodal discernment can accomplish. Equally, the approval of the revised motions testified to possibilities for a church in which bishops recognize and embrace the presence of the Spirit in the convictions and desires of the wider community of faith.[7]

---

7. For an overview of the second assembly, see Richard Lennan, "The Plenary Council as a Practice of Theology," *Australasian Catholic Record* 100 (2023): 3–24.

## Conclusion

This chapter has showcased several path-making aspects of Australia's Plenary Council, including the commitment to listen to the Spirit, the engagement with local issues, and the willingness to adjust ways of proceeding in response to "real-time" exigencies. This final section will home in on three additional trajectories from the plenary that could be instructive for the practice of synodality throughout the Catholic world.

First, effective synodal processes require a broad and deep commitment to planning, organization, and follow-up. As noted in this chapter, planning for the 2021–22 plenary began in 2018 and continued for the intervening years. Likewise, the final sets of motions from the Sydney assembly specified steps for the multiyear "implementation phase" of the plenary's decisions. A dimension of these commitments is the need to allocate financial resources to the process. In Australia's case, the financial engagement of the Australian Catholic Bishops Conference was of fundamental importance to the success of the plenary. Clearly, local churches around the world will be in different situations regarding the capacity to allocate resources to a synodal event, just as potential participants might not be free to spend a week in a synodal gathering. Planning and implementation, however, are indispensable.

Second, synodal gatherings inevitably deepen longstanding questions about roles and responsibilities in the church, especially ones where gender differences are a factor. To elaborate on this point, it will be helpful to consider the role of prayer at the plenary. Each day of the Sydney assembly began with an extended period of prayer in the assembly hall. The prayer was led often by women, and the prayer forms, art, and music used were usually contemporary. These experiences contrasted starkly with eucharistic liturgies during the week, liturgies held in the cathedral adjacent to the assembly hall. An unmissable feature of the latter was the ranks of bishops and concelebrating priests, and their separation for the plenary's other members. It is important to ask, therefore, how the church's liturgy might better reflect its synodal reality, especially in synodal gatherings. This question might elude a universally accepted answer, but it is one requiring synodal discernment.

Third, the emphasis on discernment integral to synodality underscores the ecclesial community's ongoing need for faith formation, which enriches discernment. A subtheme of this need for formation centers on how local churches promote and draw from the work of theologians. The plenary, as noted, did have a bench of theological *periti*, who contributed significantly to the development of the plenary's texts. Still, there was not always clarity about the role of theologians. Perhaps, it might well be time for a "synod on theology" to engage explicitly with this theme, which has implications for every local church.

The fact that the plenary generated questions, even as it was making a path for the immediate future of the Catholic Church in Australia, is a reminder that the church is an unfinished reality, a pilgrim people. Synodality is not a process that will instantly answer or even eliminate questions, but it does offer powerful resources for engaging those questions. These resources have their origin in grace, the life of the Holy Spirit at work through all the baptized. Australia's Plenary Council testifies vividly to the hope, enthusiasm, and sense of possibility that grace initiates and sustains.

# Bibliography

Brazal, Agnes M. "Synodality and the New Media." *Theological Studies* 84, no. 1 (2023): 95–109.

Francis, Pope. "Ceremony Commemorating the 50th Anniversary of the Institution of the Synod of Bishops." Octo-

ber 17, 2015. https://www.vatican.va/content/francesco/en/speeches/2015/october/documents/papa-francesco_20151017_50-anniversario-sinodo.html.
Lennan, Richard, Ormond Rush, Gerard Kelly, and James McEvoy. "The Plenary Council as a Practice of Theology." *Australasian Catholic Record* 100, no. 1 (2023): 3–24.
———. "Theological Reflections on the First Assembly of the Plenary Council." *Australasian Catholic Record* 99, no. 2 (2022): 131–45.
McEvoy, James Gerard. "Pope Francis on the Practice of Synodality and the Fifth Australian Plenary Council." *Theological Studies* 84, no. 1 (2023): 79–94.
Plenary Council (website). https://plenarycouncil.catholic.org.au/.
Roberto, John, ed. *Digital Ministry and Leadership in Today's Church*. Collegeville, MN: Liturgical Press, 2022.
Turman, Eboni Marshall. "The Holy Spirit and the Black Church Tradition: Womanist Considerations." In *The Holy Spirit and the Church: Ecumenical Reflections with a Pastoral Perspective*, edited by Thomas Hughson, 99–112. New York: Routledge, 2016.

# 10

# Synodality through an African Lens

## Palaver and Ubuntu

Anne Arabome, SSS

Some people may be familiar with the saying *Ex Africa semper aliquid novi*, which translates as "Out of Africa, always something new," or, "Africa always brings something new." It is attributed to—or was first quoted in Latin by—the first-century Roman naturalist, Pliny the Elder. Pliny probably did not mean it as a compliment, since he was keen to point out the oddities of African untamed natural environments that included strange interbreeding of animal species. That was a long time ago. In the intervening centuries, there has been a fairer appreciation for the values of African culture.

In this chapter, I present "palaver" as a form and practice of discernment in Africa that is well aligned with the procedures, practices, and lived experience of synodality. The primary source of the ideas presented here is African culture and calls for some nuancing. Africa is not a single entity. As a continent, Africa encompasses a variety and diversity of realities, including peoples, languages, behavior, contexts, and ways of proceeding. This diversity is stunning, and consequently, Africa is not reducible to the sum of its parts. Given this diversity, it would be impossible to characterize any concept, practice, or situation as simply representative of African culture. In any given context, culture is dynamic, evolving, and changing. Culture makes progress, and it develops in response to internal and external factors.

## Palaver, Ubuntu, and Synodality

As the theme of my contribution to this collection of tools for synodality and the procedures, practices, and lived experience that synodality entails, palaver qualifies eminently as something new out of Africa. Palaver may not be a new word to many. In fact, the idea exists in one form or another in several cultures of Africa. Etymologically, it has its roots in the Portuguese *palavra*, meaning "word." Interestingly, when one consults the dictionary meaning of palaver, one discovers that nearly all the entries have a negative meaning or connotation. They include, for example, "unnecessarily elaborate or complex procedure," "an improvised conference between two groups, typically those without a shared language or culture," "talking unproductively and at length," "talk or discussion that goes on for too long and is not important," and so on. Obviously, this brief sampling of the definitions of palaver shows that there is a linguistic bias against this word. What is of primary interest here, however, is how it can be applied to the knowledge, understanding, procedures, practices, and lived experience of synodality.

The first point to note is that palaver is none of the above dictionary definitions of the word—at least not as I understand the term and how it functions in Africa. Of course, the practice of palaver involves the spoken word; it entails talking, discussing,

# Witnesses of Synodality

conversing, dialoguing, and communicating, but it is hardly unproductive and unimportant. It is possible to consider palaver as a synonym for synodality, precisely because it entails a process of listening, engaging in dialogue, and using consultation for the purposes of discerning what the Spirit is saying to the church. This recalls the key understanding of the procedures, practices, and lived experience of synodality according to Pope Francis:

> A synodal Church is a Church which listens, which realizes that listening "is more than simply hearing." It is a mutual listening in which everyone has something to learn. The faithful people, the college of bishops, the Bishop of Rome: all listening to each other, and all listening to the Holy Spirit, the "Spirit of truth" (Jn 14:17), in order to know what he "says to the Churches" (Rev 2:7).[1]

In simple terms, palaver is a communicative practice that strives to be inclusive of the voices of all members of the community in the discussion, discernment, and resolution of matters of consequence affecting the entire community. Already, from this definition, we can see how it is rooted in another African philosophical and ethical concept, namely, ubuntu. This concept recognizes and celebrates the mutual belonging and affirmation of human beings and their natural environment. It can be formulated in various ways, one of which is, "Who I am is who we are...who we are is who I am." Or, "I am because we are." In this sense, relationality equals existence: a person is a person through and because of other people. We are not a closed entity, or, as the popular saying goes, no one is an island.

---

1. Pope Francis, "Address Commemorating the 50th Anniversary of the Institution of the Synod of Bishops," October 17, 2015, https://www.vatican.va/content/francesco/en/speeches/2015/october/documents/papa-francesco_20151017_50-anniversario-sinodo.html.

In this sense, palaver is a communal procedure, practice, and experience.

Ubuntu entails a deep understanding of the value and worth of existence situated in the wider nexus of family, community, and society. It implies that we are all connected—the unborn, the living, and the living-dead or ancestors. This connection is not cosmetic or superficial. If anything, it is existential. We survive as a community, as human beings, because we belong to one another. To paraphrase Pope Francis's teaching in *Laudato Si'*, we are all connected; everything is related, and he might add: we are saved together as members of a common family.

Within this spirit of ubuntu, there is a deep core of connection and relationality that is not only existential but also profoundly spiritual. We form a body, a community that is not static but dynamic because this body is animated by the Holy Spirit. This Spirit is alive and active in the individual members, and each member counts. In this sense, palaver connects intricately to ubuntu: nobody controls or dominates the space of conversation; the word, opinion, or voice of each member of the community counts; nobody is so unimportant as to have no word to contribute to the life of the community. Quite clearly, between palaver and ubuntu we are placed firmly in the realm of synodality, which, as we have noted, promotes journeying and walking together and listening to the Holy Spirit and to one another as the people of God, the Body of Christ, or the family of God.

## Key Elements, Dimensions, Procedures, and Processes

What are the key elements, dimensions, procedures, and processes of palaver as a practice of communal discernment in the context of synodality? There are many, but let's consider only the salient ones.

## Witnesses of Synodality

First, the practices and outcomes of palaver are neither automatic nor superficial. In reality, palaver is both a practice and a form of discernment in common. Unlike the disparaging dictionary definitions, to be engaged in palaver is to be engaged in a process of discernment that seeks a path forward for the community. This process may involve lengthy and even laborious conversation, consultation, and discussion, but it is neither pointless nor useless. Palaver calls for commitment on the part of all the participants. As a communicative process and practice of discernment, palaver unveils the hidden word or wisdom in the heart of each member of the community. More importantly, it allows the Spirit to blow wherever it wills through the members of the community. The practice of palaver as an experience of discernment calls forth an attitude of *listening*, not only to the leaders but also to the category of people that Jesus of Nazareth would have described as the least of my sisters and brothers (cf. Matt 25), that is, those who are weak and vulnerable or who consider themselves exiled from the church. Thus, palaver, as I have noted, is inclusive, just like synodality: "The vision of a Church capable of radical inclusion, shared belonging, and deep hospitality according to the teachings of Jesus is at the heart of the synodal process."[2]

Second, there are many advantages to the practice of palaver as a form of communal discernment in a synodal church. A community that engages in the communicative ethics and practice of palaver stands to gain a great deal. Speaking and listening as a community of discernment in a synodal church is healing, renewing, and liberating. It means that the word that is spoken and shared is never oppressive or violent; it is ever new, always renewed and always renewing. Think of synodality as a dynamic

---

2. "General Secretariat of the Synod, "'Enlarge the Space of Your Tent' (Is 54:2): Working Document for the Continental Stage," October 2023, no. 31, https://www.synod.va/content/dam/synod/common/phases/continental-stage/dcs/Documento-Tappa-Continentale-EN.pdf.

## Synodality through an African Lens

process of speaking and listening under the guidance and animation of the Holy Spirit. This does not mean that there will be no disagreement among the members of the community. On the contrary, palaver allows all the viewpoints, no matter how divergent and controversial, to be brought forward with the aim of achieving a consensus. A community that practices this kind of process can never be static, stale, or staid, because the word never rests, and the Holy Spirit is never dormant. As Scripture says, "Indeed, the word of God is living and active, sharper than any two-edged sword, piercing until it divides soul from spirit, joints from marrow; it is able to judge the thoughts and intentions of the heart" (Heb 4:12). Such is the power of the African understanding and practice of palaver and its relevance as a practice and experience of synodality!

Third, the practice of palaver is always a widening circle of conversation, relationality, and engagements. Nobody is left out or left behind. This practice captures the essence of synodality: "For this reason, while all the baptized are specifically called to take part in the Synodal Process, no one—no matter their religious affiliation—should be excluded from sharing their perspective and experiences, insofar as they want to help the Church on her synodal journey of seeking what is good and true. This is especially true of those who are most vulnerable or marginalized."[3] Similarly, as Pope Francis states, "when our hearts are authentically open to universal communion, this sense of fraternity excludes nothing and no one."[4] This inclusive nature of palaver offers the church an important tool for organizing synodal moments in a way that maximizes the collective

---

3. General Secretariat of the Synod, "Vademecum for the Synod on Synodality: Official Handbook for Listening and Discernment in Local Churches," September 7, 2021, https://www.synod.va/en/news/the-vademecum-for-the-synod-on-synodality.html.

4. Pope Francis, "Encyclical Letter on the Care for our Common Home, *Laudato Si'*," May 24, 2015, no. 92, https://www.vatican.va/content/francesco/en/encyclicals/documents/papa-francesco_20150524_enciclica-laudato-si.html.

## Witnesses of Synodality

wisdom, depth, and experience that lies in the community to promote communion, participation, and mission in the church.

Given the flaws of social organization that create various kinds of inequalities, palaver may not always function as ideally as it should. In some instances, including within the church, the voices and participation of some people may be suppressed, hindered, or excluded for a variety of reasons. But the ideal of palaver remains important—it calls us forth to strive constantly and consistently for an inclusive practice of conversation and discernment as a body, especially as the Body of Christ, the people of God, and the family of God.

In the spirit of synodality, palaver as a practice of communal discernment entails the idea of solidarity. In society, as we find in the church, there are women and men, rich and poor, young and old, healthy and infirm, and weak and powerful people. Palaver creates a common ground for all to meet. Like synodality, palaver gives a voice and a word to each person. To stifle or impede this word amounts to obstructing the action and the work of the Holy Spirit in the church. In this form of communal discernment, every member is an essential part of the process, based on their baptismal dignity as children of God and the people of God.

Fourth, as should be clear by now, the palaver circle is open-ended. For this reason, it is often imagined as a dialogical experience that happens under a tree. In other words, it creates a boundless space—ever widening and always including more participants in the extraordinary desire to achieve consensus and overcome division with reconciliation and mutual understanding. Although palaver refers to a word that is spoken and shared, this is not the only medium of communication. Like the Holy Spirit who blows wherever she wills, palaver can take various forms, including dance, storytelling, mime, mythology, and even silence. The last of these is important: not every word is spoken and listening in silence is often the most creative disposition in the context of palaver as a process of discernment. To listen is more important than imposing one's viewpoints on others.

Consequently, the basic premise of palaver as a practice of discernment in a communicative framework is *truth*. The Spirit of God guarantees truth, and to find and live or practice this truth, the community must be open to the Holy Spirit communicating truth through its members. The paramount nature of this fact cannot be overstated. The aim of palaver is to establish truth that will sustain the common good. Like synodality, the Holy Spirit makes this possible, because the action of the Holy Spirit is not tied to the status of members of the community. The action of the Holy Spirit spreads peace, understanding, love, harmony, and forbearance in the community.

On a local level, the community can engage in palaver in any context. This recalls the practice of synodality, especially as Pope Francis has defined it: it is a grassroots process. It begins in the local churches—in families, neighborhoods, small Christian communities, parishes, and dioceses. It is not the preserve of the ordained clergy or of bishops. It is a space of discernment of the people of God, by the people of God, and for the people of God. According to Pope Francis, "It is important that the synodal process be exactly this: a process of becoming, a process that involves the local Churches, in different phases and from the bottom-up, in an exciting and engaging effort that can forge a style of communion and participation directed to mission."[5]

## Palaver and Synodality in Action

I have been privileged to participate in and facilitate several synodal events in Africa that used this method of palaver.

---

5. Pope Francis, "Address on the Occasion of the Moment of Reflection for the Beginning of the Synodal Journey," October 9, 2021, https://press.vatican.va/content/salastampa/en/bollettino/pubblico/2021/10/09/211009a.html.

## Witnesses of Synodality

Although I was not present for the African Synodal Continental Assembly that took place in Addis Ababa, Ethiopia, under the auspices of the Symposium of Episcopal Conferences of Africa and Madagascar (SECAM), it illustrates how this practice of palaver functions as a moment of synodality. From March 1 to 6, 2023, 209 delegates gathered in Addis Ababa for the final moment of the continental phase of the synod on synodality. The composition of the assembly was marked by diversity: the event was an ecclesial gathering of the people of God from all over Africa, including laywomen and -men, religious women and men, young people, priests, bishops, and representatives of other Christian traditions and other faith traditions. All those present at the assembly participated in equal measure without anyone being excluded or prevented from contributing to the conversation in the community of the people of God. The process was marked by dialogue, mutual listening, and discernment in common, using the methodology of spiritual conversation. The assembly focused on matters of critical importance to the church in Africa.

The final official communiqué of the SECAM Assembly described the experience as a moment that highlighted the African way of palaver:[6]

> With courage and joy, confidence and humility, we listened to one another and to the Holy Spirit. In a spirit of discernment, we listened to what the People of God from around the world said in the first year of the Synod. In prayer and silence, we discerned the intuitions, discussed the questions and themes and identified the calls of our synodal journey in order

---

6. Symposium of Episcopal Conferences of Africa and Madagascar, "In Africa, the Synod Is On!" Final Communiqué of the Africa Synodal Continental Assembly, March 1–6, 2023, https://secam.org/in-africa-the-synod-is-on/.

## Synodality through an African Lens

to prepare an African Synodal Document that represents the authentic voice of Africa. The time we have spent together has been an experience of lived synodality—a moment of profound dialogue, listening and discernment among local churches and with the Universal Church.

Africa is a synodal continent. Synodality is part of who we are and how we live as the Family of God in Africa. Our continent is blessed with rich principles and values of our cultures and traditions. Indeed, rooted in African anthropological principles and cultural values, especially Palaver, Ubuntu and Ujamaa,[7] which emphasize community spirit, sense of family, teamwork, solidarity, inclusivity, hospitality and conviviality, the Catholic Church in Africa has grown as a Family of God. These principles and values are good and healthy seeds for the birth and growth of a truly synodal Church in Africa and in the world.

This account demonstrates that palaver is not just a theory but a practical tool for realizing the goals, objectives, and purposes of synodality. It is a gift to the synodal church.

As already noted, the practice of palaver as a form of discernment is triadic in nature as it involves the living members of the community and the Holy Spirit—and all of these with nature. Palaver strengthens the circle of life and restores and enhances relationships while cementing the bond of shared humanity among all the constituent elements of community and nature.

---

7. *Ujamaa* is Swahili for "family" and "familyhood." Like ubuntu, it connotes a sense of belonging and a life of shared purpose and meaning in community.

# Witnesses of Synodality

## Conclusion

In conclusion, how can the African tradition of palaver and the spirit of ubuntu that it is rooted in inspire the Catholic Church's current synodal renewal? First, synodality requires a deep commitment to listening, dialogue, and discernment. From the foregoing, the practice of synodality is a shared process of listening, dialogue, and discernment of what the Spirit is saying to the church. At the conclusion of this journey is the truth of the word of God. Thus, as a practice, procedure, and lived experience of communal discernment and synodality, the purpose of palaver is to deepen, promote, and sustain the growth of the essential life force of the community. At the heart of the process of synodality—its procedures, practices, and lived experience—is the willingness and commitment to listen. Pope Francis confirms this when he asserts,

> We need a respectful, mutual listening, free of ideology and predetermined agendas. The aim is not to reach agreement by means of a contest between opposing positions, but to journey together to seek God's will, allowing differences to harmonize. Most important of all is the synodal spirit: to meet each other with respect and trust, to believe in our shared unity, and to receive the new thing that the Spirit wishes to reveal to us.[8]

In this way, the gifts of the Holy Spirit are encouraged not only to blossom but to overcome the darkness that is part of our human nature and to invite the light of our common humanity

---

8. Austen Ivereigh, *Let Us Dream: The Path to a Better Future; Pope Francis in Conversation with Austen Ivereigh* (London: Simon & Schuster, 2020), 93.

to shine forth. Understood as such, palaver offers us an example of the practice of communal discernment and a model of lived synodality in the life of the people of God, the church.

Second, synodality thrives in an environment of respectful, inclusive, and purposeful dialogue. The goals and purposes of synodality depend largely on the willingness and commitment of the church as people of God to create the space where it can flourish as a habitual way of proceeding. As the church continues the synodal journey, palaver will serve as a key component of the procedures, practices, and lived experience of synodality. For this to happen, it would be important for the church at all levels to create the conducive environment for the People of God to gather, to listen to one another without any member feeling excluded; to engage in dialogue and conversation about matters that affect the ecclesial community; and to discern with clarity what the Holy Spirit is saying to the community, in particular, and to the church, in general.

## Bibliography

African Synodality Initiative. *A Pocket Companion to Synodality: Voices from Africa*. Nairobi: African Synodality Initiative Jesuit Conference of Africa and Madagascar, 2022.

Andraos, Michel, Thierry-Marie Courau, and Carlos Mendoza Álvarez, eds. *Concilium: International Journal for Theology 2021/2; Synodalities*. Norwich: SCM Press, 2021.

General Secretariat of the Synod. "'Enlarge the Space of Your Tent' (Is 54:2): Working Document for the Continental Stage." October 2023. https://www.synod.va/content/dam/synod/common/phases/continental-stage/dcs/Documento-Tappa-Continentale-EN.pdf.

## Witnesses of Synodality

———. "Vademecum for the Synod on Synodality: Official Handbook for Listening and Discernment in Local Churches." September 7, 2021. https://www.synod.va/en/news/the-vademecum-for-the-synod-onsynodality.html.

Ivereigh, Austen. *Let Us Dream: The Path to a Better Future; Pope Francis in Conversation with Austen Ivereigh*. London: Simon & Schuster, 2020.

Pope Francis. "Address Commemorating the 50th Anniversary of the Institution of the Synod of Bishops." October 17, 2015. https://www.vatican.va/content/francesco/en/speeches/2015/october/documents/papa-francesco_20151017_50-anniversario-sinodo.html.

———. "Address on the Occasion of the Moment of Reflection for the Beginning of the Synodal Journey." October 9, 2021. https://press.vatican.va/content/salastampa/en/bollettino/pubblico/2021/10/09/211009a.html.

———. "Encyclical Letter on the Care for Our Common Home, *Laudato Si'*." May 24, 2015. https://www.vatican.va/content/francesco/en/encyclicals/documents/papa-francesco_20150524_enciclica-laudato-si.html.

Symposium of Episcopal Conferences of Africa and Madagascar. "In Africa, the Synod Is On!" Final Communiqué of the Africa Synodal Continental Assembly. March 1–6, 2023. https://secam.org/in-africa-the-synod-is-on/.

# 11

# Synodality in a Continental Perspective

## Latin America and the Caribbean

*Birgit Weiler, MMS*

Since the 1950s, the Church in Latin America and the Caribbean has developed a strong practice of conciliar, synodal, and collegial ways of walking together as the people of God.[1] It started in 1955 with the creation of the Consejo Episcopal Latinoamericano y Caribeño: the Episcopal Council of Latin America and the Caribbean (CELAM). The council was founded by the Holy See at the request of the region's bishops. While the initial purpose was to foster "communion, reflection, collaboration and service" among the bishops, over time it has become more

---

1. Cf. "Synthesis of the Continental Stage of the Synod in Latin America and the Caribbean," April 2023, no. 18: "The conciliar, synodal and collegial life in our Church has a long history." Full text at https://www.synod.va/content/dam/synod/common/phases/continental-stage/final_document/celam.pdf.

## Witnesses of Synodality

inclusive.[2] The collegial process, started in 1955, includes various CELAM meetings, the Amazon Synod in 2019, the Ecclesial Assembly for Latin America and the Caribbean in 2021, and the recent listening process for the 2021–2024 Synod on Synodality.

In this chapter, we examine nearly seven decades of Latin American synodality, with a special focus on the following questions: What have the people of God of this region contributed to the synodal process, and what have we learned in the process? In doing so, I gratefully draw on my experiences as a participant in the Amazon Synod, the 2021 Ecclesial Assembly, and the process leading up to the Latin American Synthesis for the Synod 2021–2024.

## Five "General Episcopal Conferences"

CELAM was founded at the First General Episcopal Conference in Rio de Janeiro in 1955. It was the first time that bishops from a continent had held such a gathering. The ecclesial practice of walking together continued and intensified through four subsequent conferences. The meeting in Medellin (1968) marked the reception of Vatican II in Latin America and is known for its affirmation of the preferential option for the poor that was further developed by the Conferences of Puebla (1979), Santo Domingo (1992), and Aparecida (2007).

Though these were episcopal conferences and, therefore, only bishops spoke and voted on the final document, they, in fact, featured several participatory elements. For example, before a conference, CELAM always circulated a Preparatory Document for broad consultation. Many small Christian communities (also called base communities), other Christian movements, and

---

2. On its home page, CELAM states, "El Consejo Episcopal Latinoamericano (CELAM) es un organismo de comunión, reflexión, colaboración y servicio," https://celam.org/celam/.

## Synodality in a Continental Perspective

parishes responded with commentaries, insights, and proposals. Moreover, bishops were usually accompanied by theological advisors who participated actively in producing reflections and texts for the final documents of the conferences.

These five General Episcopal Conferences were characterized by close attention to the signs of the times, a careful and collective discernment of these signs in light of the gospel, and an interest in discovering God's will for the life and mission of the church in the current context. The Latin American and Caribbean Church's way of reflecting, therefore, shows remarkable continuity with the process of the current Synod 2021–2024.

## The Amazon Synod

The Amazon Synod (2019) was a milestone on the path toward greater synodality, especially because approximately twenty-five thousand people from various parts of the Amazon region participated in its preparatory phase. They included people with different vocations and ministries in the Amazonian Church, as well as people who do not identify as Christians but who share the church's commitment to an integral ecology in Amazonia. In a process of listening to one another, these people discerned, with the assistance of God's Spirit, "new paths for the Church and for an Integral Ecology" in Amazonia.[3] There was a special emphasis on facilitating the participation of groups who have historically been marginalized and whose voices have generally not been heard, especially Indigenous or original peoples and communities of African descent (*quilombos*).

At the synod, which took place in Rome, the active participation of Indigenous women and men on behalf of their

---

3. Cf. "Final Document of the Amazon Synod," Special Assembly of the Synod of Bishops for the Pan-Amazon Region, "Amazonia: New Paths for the Church and for an Integral Ecology," October 6–27, 2019, http://secretariat.synod.va/content/sinodoamazonico/en/documents/final-document-of-the-amazon-synod.html.

communities was a historical moment for the entire church. It sharpened awareness of the truth that growing in synodality requires being ready to accept the rich cultural diversity in our church. The Final Document of the Amazon Synod reflects key insights into the nature of synodality and what it requires. For example, it states, "In order to walk together, the Church today needs a conversion to the synodal experience."[4] What also increased was the awareness that synodality implies being open to the cry of the earth and the cry of the poor.[5]

Afterward, the Amazon Synod inspired the creation of a new synodal body of governance, the Ecclesial Conference of the Amazon (Conferencia Eclesial de la Amazonía, or CEAMA). It was intentionally designed, not as a conference of bishops but as a leadership body that consists of bishops, priests, laymen and -women, and religious men and women. CEAMA was the first ecclesial body of this kind, and, as such, it was very much learning by doing a synodal practice of leadership. The Amazon Synod also played an important role in inspiring a renewal and restructuring of CELAM, so it could better foster the development of a synodal church in Latin America and the Caribbean.

## The Ecclesial Assembly of Latin America and the Caribbean

Another landmark was the First Ecclesial Assembly of Latin America and the Caribbean. In 2019, Pope Francis had encouraged the region's bishops to take a more synodal approach by holding an assembly rather than a sixth CELAM general conference. While the latter would have been mainly a gathering of bishops, an ecclesial assembly allowed for broader and more

---

4. "Final Document of the Amazon Synod," no. 88
5. "Final Document of the Amazon Synod," no. 10.

diverse participation. Again, this was the first assembly of its kind. Because of the COVID-19 pandemic, the ecclesial assembly was postponed till 2021.

In preparation for the assembly and despite the restrictions imposed by the pandemic, more than seventy thousand people participated in a listening process modeled after the one for the Amazon Synod, but this time the process was more extensive. Its purpose was to discern together the current signs of the time in Latin America and the Caribbean and to respond to them as a church called to incarnate herself in this context.

The First Ecclesial Assembly was held in a hybrid form in Mexico. Listening continued to be a main characteristic. During the assembly, about one hundred groups met online for community discernment. The organizers had ensured that each group included people from different cultures, countries, age groups, genders, vocations, charisms, ministries, and services within the church. In a short reflection on the contribution of the ecclesial assembly to the Synod 2021–2024 process, the 2023 Continental Synthesis calls the ecclesial assembly "a real milestone," as it "combines the participation of many members of the people of God with the bishops' practice of pastoral ministry."[6]

CELAM's Pastoral-Theological Reflection Team gathered the contributions from the listening and discernment processes before and during the ecclesial assembly and drafted a text to guide the assembly's implementation, with the title *Hacia una Iglesia sinodal en salida hacia las periferias: Reflexiones y propuestas pastorales a partir de la Primera Asamblea Eclesial de América Latina y el Caribe* (Toward a synodal church that goes out to the peripheries: Reflections and proposals from the First Ecclesial Assembly of Latin America and the Caribbean).[7]

---

6. CELAM, "Synthesis of the Continental Stage of the Synod in Latin America and the Caribbean," no. 20.

7. Full text at https://asambleaeclesial.lat/wp-content/uploads/2022/10/ingles.pdf.

## Witnesses of Synodality

During the ecclesial assembly, the church in this region learned to acknowledge the need for greater inclusion of women and young people in ecclesial decision-making and decision taking, an important learning experience. This had been emphasized by many participants, including priests and bishops in the listening process prior to the assembly. The process of the ecclesial assembly led to a heightened awareness and sensitivity that has resulted in more just and inclusive procedures and practices in many Latin American episcopal conferences.

In numerous dioceses in Latin America and the Caribbean, priests, especially diocesan priests, are reluctant to commit themselves to synodal processes. Many of them sense a lack of clarity regarding the identity, ministry, and role of the priest in a synodal church. They fear that these aspects will suffer from synodality. Experience is teaching us that it is very important to create and sustain spaces of mutual listening and discernment for priests, in which fears and doubts can be freely expressed and that allow for shared reflection about what it means to be a priest in a synodal church. In these reflections, the testimony and thoughts of priests who already live their priesthood in a synodal spirit are very valuable.

# The Synod on Synodality: The Continental Stage

Because of the experience gained in the preparatory processes for the Synod for the Amazon and the ecclesial assembly, the people of God in Latin America and the Caribbean were well prepared for the Synod 2021–2024 and the active participation it calls for. As in other places, the local listening process was followed by a continental stage. In consultation with the local bishops, CELAM facilitated the broad participation of men and women representing the different vocations and ministries in

## Synodality in a Continental Perspective

our church. Meetings were held in the four geographic regions that are part of CELAM's organizational structure: San Salvador (El Salvador) for the Central American region and Mexico (CAMEX), Santo Domingo (Dominican Republic) for the Caribbean region; Quito (Ecuador) for the Bolivarian region (Bolivia, Colombia, Ecuador, Peru, and Venezuela), and Brasília (Brazil) for the Southern Cone region. Those meetings drew over four hundred participants, nearly half of them laypeople, representing diverse charisms and ministries, as well as the ethnic, cultural, and social diversity that characterizes the Latin American and Caribbean Church.

Especially positive was the fact that, in convening these regional meetings, particular attention was given to the inclusion of the voices of people living in poverty and of those who are marginalized or excluded for social, ethnic, cultural, and gender reasons, as well as the voices of people working with groups at the margins, like those in prison, migrants, refugees, and persons with disabilities or special gifts.

Less present in this group are believers from other Christian denominations and other religions. In Latin America, ecumenical or interfaith collaboration is often still viewed with fear, even by groups that respect one another and are sincerely interested in responding together to the urgent challenges of our time. There is even greater fear of people who identify as agnostic, atheist, or having no bonds with an organized religion. This certainly needs to be a point of attention.

All the regional meetings began with a retreat day that helped create an attitude of deep personal listening to the voice of God in scripture, in personal and communal prayer, in liturgical celebrations, and in the voices of the sisters and brothers, particularly during the times of communal discernment. Much attention was also given to elements that facilitated integral prayer, involving not only the mind but also the heart and the body, with its different senses.

### Witnesses of Synodality

At the beginning of the regional meetings, a specific method of spiritual conversation was introduced that focused on active listening and personal and communal discernment. (Many participants had also taken part in the ecclesial assembly and were familiar with this spiritual practice.) The method helped participants listen with openness, attending to what others communicated both verbally and nonverbally, free from preconceived ideas and personal agendas.

Nevertheless, several participants also commented on a weak point of this method, namely that it does not allow for reflection on arguments. Yet presenting arguments on issues that arise—and that may be contentious—and reflection on their strengths and weaknesses also seems important for discernment. For future synodal processes, it will be helpful to develop this aspect.

## CELAM Contributions to the Synod on Synodality

After the regional meetings, the next step was to draft a synthesis of the input from those meetings. This happened at a meeting from March 17 to 20, 2023, with representatives of various groups: CELAM's Center for Pastoral Action Programs and Networks (Centro de Programas y Redes de Acción Pastoral, CEPRAP), the Ecclesial Conference of the Amazon (CEAMA), the Confederation of Latin American and Caribbean Religious (CLAR), and members of CELAM's Pastoral-Theological Reflection Team. All of us who participated experienced the spiritual conversation method as fruitful, for it helped us to treasure the contributions in their diversity. Out of respect for these contributions and to honor the voices of the participants themselves, we included in the synthesis many quotations from the regional

## Synodality in a Continental Perspective

meetings. In what follows I will list some key contributions from those meetings.

First, participants identified the need for a change of mentality and structure. As the synthesis reads, "synodality requires a personal, community, ecclesial and structural conversion (Southern Cone), and therefore a change of mentality and a change of structures (Camex) is urgently needed."[8] These dimensions of conversion, mentality, and structure are interwoven; structural reform is necessary to facilitate the practice of synodality. Participants observed that "a new synodal ecclesiality" is emerging that "places us before the challenge of imagining new structures. Some have already been emerging, such as the Ecclesial Conference for the Amazon (CEAMA) and the First Ecclesial Assembly of Latin America and the Caribbean" (no. 81). The new structures must be incarnated in the different realities. It also became clear that the implementation of structural reforms to facilitate greater participation cannot depend solely on the good will of a particular church authority (parish priest, bishop, etc.) but demands a "reform of the Code of Canon Law" (Bolivarian region) (no. 81).

New structures "place us before forms of organization and functioning that must see how to articulate the sense of faith of all the faithful, episcopal authority, and the service of theology, because the Holy Spirit speaks through all the people of God as a whole and not only through some—the bishops—or only one—the Bishop of Rome, who has primacy" (no. 81). Thus, "if the People of God were not a subject in decision making, there is no synodality" (CEAMA-REPAM) (no. 81).

Second, based on many contributions, the synthesis speaks of a "deformation of the ministry in the abuse of power." It emphasizes "the need to think of a conversion within the church

---

8. CELAM, "Synthesis of the Continental Stage of the Synod in Latin America and the Caribbean," no. 73. The remaining notes in this section all come from this Synthesis.

## Witnesses of Synodality

that overcomes the clericalism and machismo that exclude women from discernment and decision-making processes." At the same time, it recognizes that "this is something cultural that we must face, even if we have to go against the current. Fraternity and sisterhood are what we must cultivate" (Cono Sur-REPAM) (no. 87). It was stressed by many that the 2023 synod should deepen these themes: "The leadership of women and their contribution in theological reflection, in pastoral councils, in the accompaniment of communities, in the areas of elaboration and decision-making" (no. 39). The women's diaconate was also mentioned explicitly: "Many voices consider the institution of the diaconate for women urgent; it is a way to recognize what is already the lived reality of several communities" (no. 86).

Third, the Latin American and Caribbean Church seeks to be more inclusive. The synthesis document states that Jesus's spirit calls all of us "to include the poor, LGBTQIA+ communities, couples in a second union," and others who do not feel accepted in the church (no. 65). Young people in particular call for "listening, integration, and participation in decision-making in the Church" (no. 70).

Fourth, the synthesis dedicated the fifth chapter to a "socio-environmental commitment in a fragmented world." During the regional meetings, we became aware, in a self-critical spirit, of "the distance of [many] local Churches...from the peripheries" (Southern Cone) (no. 64). The synthesis reflects the insistence of many participants that a synodal church is called to "go out from herself and to place herself, with all her mission, at the service of society" (no. 63). Several contributions highlighted the urgent need to heed "the cry of the peoples and the earth" as this "is a commitment to the Gospel, which calls us to be allies of the peoples in the defense of their life and their territories" (Southern Cone), particularly in Amazonia (no. 67). For many, learning to live synodality means learning to be a church ready "to walk with those who serve the suffering, to seek alternatives to the throwaway culture, and to confront the various forms of violence that have increased in recent years" (no. 66).

Fifth, the participants spoke about the prevention of abuse in all its forms. Admittedly, it took the Church in Latin America and the Caribbean some time to overcome its resistance to acknowledging sexual abuse and abuses of power and conscience, to stand with those affected by abuses perpetrated by priests and other members of the church, and to strive for justice and reparation. Until recently, church leaders were virtually silent about this topic, and public recognition of the extent of the issue is still lacking. The synthesis states clearly that in a synodal church, "the formation of a culture of respect for all persons and the prevention of any kind of abuse must be a transversal axis in all aspects of church life" (no. 78).

## Conclusion

The Church in Latin America and the Caribbean is already seventy years on the way to greater synodality and thus greater communion, participation, and mission. Many active Catholics in this region recognize with joy, gratitude, and hope that a synodal church is emerging.[9] Especially through the method of spiritual conversation used recently, the Church in Latin America and the Caribbean has renewed its understanding that all baptized people are fully members of the people of God and therefore are called to practice their *sensus fidei* in co-responsibility for the life and mission of the church.[10] In communal discernment,

---

9. See Daniel De Ycaza and Mauricio López, "The Latin American Church's Synodal Conversion: Walking Together from Blindness to Light," *La Civiltà Cattolica* (March 24, 2023), https://www.laciviltacattolica.com/the-latin-american-churchs-synodal-conversion/.

10. See "Synthesis of the Continental Stage of the Synod in Latin America and the Caribbean," no. 96. See also Rafael Luciani, *Synodality: A New Way of Proceeding in the Church* (Mahwah, NJ: Paulist Press, 2022).

## Witnesses of Synodality

awareness has grown strong that the Spirit is the protagonist in this process and that all are called to be open to the surprises of God's creative *Ruah* (Spirit). She blows where she wills and encourages the faithful to explore and walk new roads. God's Spirit calls for a communal conversion and transformation, acting "clearly from below, from the poor in society and in the Church."[11]

In conclusion, I share some significant insights and lessons learned from CELAM's ongoing effort to foster synodality that may be helpful in our common quest for a more synodal church.

First, we must remain open to God's creative Spirit, the protagonist of ongoing personal and communal conversion. Spiritual discernment is a key element of the synodal process, in general, and the synodal method of spiritual conversation, in particular. This requires practice in daily prayer, spiritual accompaniment, retreats, and meetings. Continuous self-examination and examination in the group regarding the following questions is crucial: How are we listening to each other and to God's Spirit working in us and among us? How do we handle different viewpoints and the tensions they might cause? In those cases, how do we listen to the Spirit as protagonist in the synodal process?

Second, formation is important. A comprehensive introduction to the method of spiritual conversation is essential. Those who facilitate the complex processes of community discernment need careful, integral preparation. Experience in the regional meetings showed that the discernment process is far more fruitful when guided by well-prepared facilitators.

Third, to truly listen in a synodal spirit, we need to include those who are marginalized in our societies and church. Therefore, it is essential to ask regularly, whose voices are missing at

---

11. Victor Codina, "El Espíritu actúa desde abajo: Pneumatología desde América Latina," Teologica Latinoamericana Enciclopédia Digital, published online at: https://teologicalatinoamericana.com/?p=1135. For more extensive reflection, see Victor Codina, *El Espíritu del Señor actúa desde abajo* (Santander: Sal Terrae, 2015).

## Synodality in a Continental Perspective

our table of listening, dialoguing, and discerning? Whom else would we like to invite? Who could help us to contact those who are still missing?

Fourth, becoming an authentically synodal church requires a change of mentality. Besides cultivating an attitude of active listening, dialogue, and discernment, a systematic, integral, and ongoing formation in synodality for all members of the people of God is indispensable. It helps significantly when the input is outlined and presented by a team of men and women who are formed in fields such as theology, spirituality, pastoral care, communication, and so on, and who also represent different vocations and ministries within the church. Such a team can help foster the change of mentality needed to overcome clericalism, machismo, and "clerical authoritarianism."[12]

Finally, the change of mentality must go hand in hand with a change of structures. Synodality needs structures that foster strong lay participation, especially by women and young people, in decision-making and decision-taking. During the synodal consultations, it was helpful to identify structures that already exist in some local churches and consider their feasibility in other ecclesial contexts. The examples were inspirational for the creation of synodal structures in various contexts.

With the eyes of faith, one can read the entire process toward greater synodality in Latin America and the Caribbean that has been fostered and accompanied by CELAM as the ongoing work of God's creative Spirit. The Spirit is leading the church in recognizing the great theological and ecclesiological significance of the people of God in the church and its mission. This encourages us to continue the synodal journey with profound trust in God's Spirit and his transforming love.

---

12. "Synthesis of the Continental Stage of the Synod in Latin America and the Caribbean," no. 87.

# Bibliography

CELAM. "Synthesis of the Continental Stage of the Synod in Latin America and the Caribbean." April 2023. https://www.synod.va/content/dam/synod/common/phases/continental-stage/final_document/celam.pdf.

Codina, Victor. "El Espíritu actúa desde abajo: Pneumatología desde América Latina." Teologica Latinoamericana Enciclopédia Digital. https://teologicalatinoamericana.com/?p=1135.

———. *El Espíritu del Señor actúa desde abajo*. Santander: Sal Terrae, 2015.

De Ycaza, Daniel, and Mauricio López. "The Latin American Church's Synodal Conversion: Walking Together from Blindness to Light," *La Civiltà Cattolica* (March 24, 2023): https://www.laciviltacattolica.com/the-latin-american-churchs-synodal-conversion/.

"Final Document of the Amazon Synod." Special Assembly of the Synod of Bishops for the Pan-Amazon Region, "Amazonia: New Paths for the Church and for an Integral Ecology," October 6–27, 2019. http://secretariat.synod.va/content/sinodoamazonico/en/documents/final-document-of-the-amazon-synod.html.

Luciani, Rafael. *Synodality: A New Way of Proceeding in the Church*. Mahwah, NJ: Paulist Press, 2022.

# About the Contributors

## Anne Arabome

Anne Arabome is a Sister of Social Service. She serves as the associate director of the Faber Center for Ignatian Spirituality at Marquette University (USA). Her recent publications include *Why Do You Trouble This Woman? Women and the Spiritual Exercises of St. Ignatius of Loyola* (Paulist Press, 2022).

## Laure Blanchon

Laure Blanchon is an Ursuline sister of the Roman Union. She is a professor of dogmatic and practical theology at the Facultés Loyola Paris (France) and she coordinates the Constitutions Commission of her institute. Her recent publications include "Revisiter la vie en Eglise à l'école des plus pauvres," in *Les derniers seront les premiers: La parole des pauvres dans le processus synodal* (Emmanuel, 2022), and "Une Eglise à l'écoute des pauvres et du peuple de Dieu," in *Les grands chantiers du pape François* (Facultés jésuites de Paris, 2023).

# Witnesses of Synodality

## Brian Flanagan

Brian Flanagan is a theologian, senior fellow at New Ways Ministry, and past president of the College Theology Society. Most recently, he was associate professor of theology at Marymount University (USA). He is the author of *Stumbling in Holiness: Sin and Sanctity in the Church* (Liturgical Press, 2017), and "Reception in North America," in *The Oxford Handbook on Vatican II* (Oxford University Press, 2023).

## John E. Hurley

John Hurley is a Paulist father. In collaboration with Cardinal McElroy (San Diego) he coordinated two synodal gatherings in response to *Amoris Laetitia* (2016) and *Christus Vivit* (2019) and continues as a consultant to the ongoing Diocesan Synod Commission. He also works as a consultant and missionary at New Evangelization Strategies.

## Austen Ivereigh

Austen Ivereigh is a British writer known for his two biographies of Pope Francis, *The Great Reformer: Francis and the Making of a Radical Pope* (2014), and *Wounded Shepherd: Pope Francis and His Struggle to Convert the Catholic Church* (2019), and a book written in collaboration with him: *Let Us Dream: The Path to a Better Future* (2020). He is a fellow in contemporary church history at Campion Hall, Oxford. He has been involved in the synod on synodality in various roles, and he took part in the synod assembly in Rome in October 2023 as an "expert/facilitator."

About the Contributors

## Richard Lennan

Richard Lennan, a priest of the diocese of Maitland-Newcastle (Australia), was a member of the theological panel for Australia's Plenary Council. He is professor of systematic theology in the School of Theology and Ministry at Boston College. His most recent book is *Tilling the Church: Theology for an Unfinished Project* (Liturgical Press, 2022).

## Stefan Mangnus

Stefan Mangnus is a Dominican priest. He works as a pastoral supervisor and lecturer in systematic theology at Tilburg University (The Netherlands). His recent publications include *The Divinity of the Word: Thomas Aquinas Dividing and Reading the Gospel of John* (Peeters, 2022), and "Manifestation and Encounter: Revelation as Encounter in Christoph Theobald and Thomas Aquinas," in *The Enduring Significance of Thomas Aquinas* (Peeters, 2023).

## Marie-Dominique Minassian

Marie-Dominique Minassian works as a researcher at the University of Fribourg (Switzerland). She heads the scientific committee in charge of publishing the writings of the monks of Tibhirine. Her publications include Frère Luc, *Tu verras éclater le printemps: Lettres de Tibhirine* (Lettres vol. 1) (Editions du Cerf, 2021); *Heureux ceux qui osent la rencontre: Des moines en pays d'Islam* (Écrits de Tibhirine, vol. 3) (Editions du Cerf, 2022); *Heureux ceux qui accueillent: Vivre l'hospitalité* (Écrits de Tibhirine, vol. 4) (Editions du Cerf, 2023).

# Witnesses of Synodality

## Jos Moons

Jos Moons is a Jesuit priest. He works as a postdoctoral researcher and lecturer at KU Leuven (Belgium). He is the author of *The Art of Spiritual Direction: A Guide to Ignatian Practice* (Paulist Press, 2021), *The Holy Spirit, the Church, and Pneumatological Renewal: Mystici Corporis, Lumen Gentium and Beyond* (Brill, 2022), and "The Holy Spirit as the Protagonist of the Synod: Pope Francis's Creative Reception of the Second Vatican Council," *Theological Studies* 84, no. 1 (2023).

## Noel Muscat

Noel Muscat is a Franciscan friar from Malta. He has lectured Franciscan theology in Jerusalem and is currently the librarian and archivist of the Franciscan Province of Malta. His publications include a translation of the *Vita Brevior* of St. Francis by Thomas of Celano in Maltese (2016), *Melita Illyrica and Melita Africana: The Islands of St. Paul* (2018), and a history of the Franciscan presence in the sanctuaries of the Holy Land in Maltese (2021).

## Armida Veglio

Armida Veglio is an Ursuline sister of the Roman Union. She is based in Desenzano (Italy), where she is responsible for welcoming visitors to the house where the founder, Angela Merici, lived the first part of her life. She gives sessions on Saint Angela and her spirituality.

About the Contributors

# Birgit Weiler

Birgit Weiler is a Medical Mission Sister. She works as a professor and researcher at the Pontifical Catholic University of Peru (PUCP), and she is a member of the Team for Theological Reflection at the Episcopal Council of Latin America and the Caribbean (CELAM). Her publications include "Escuchar el grito de los pobres y el clamor de la tierra: Ecología integral desde la Amazonía," in *Los signos de este tiempo: Fundamentos, mediaciones y discernimientos* (Universidad Alberto Hurtado, 2022), and "Synodalität kultivieren: In Leben und Struktur der Kirche von Amazonien wie der Weltkirche," in *Laboratorium Weltkirche: Die Amazonien-Synode und ihre Potenziale* (Herder, 2022).

# Rebekka Willekes

Rebekka Willekes is a Cistercian nun. She is the prioress of the monastery of Our Lady of Klaarland in Belgium.

Other Books Published by Paulist Press

## Just Church
### Catholic Social Teaching, Synodality, and Women
*Phyllis Zagano*

*Just Church* engages the reader in the synodal pathway to a "Just Church" that can and should reflect its social teaching. An important measure of justice is an ecclesiology open to participation by others beyond celibate clerics, especially in consideration of competing Catholic ecclesial bodies and methods of membership.

978-0-8091-5653-5   $17.95

Other Books Published by Paulist Press

# Synodality
A New Way of Proceeding in the Church
*Rafael Luciani*
FOREWORD BY
*Peter Hünermann*

Synodality envisions a new way of proceeding in the Church: toward a coresponsible and participatory Church for the third millennium. It is an ecclesial model that calls for the recognition of laity as full subjects in the Church.

978-0-8091-5611-5    $18.95

Other Books Published by Paulist Press

# Reforming the Church
## A Synodal Way of Proceeding
### *Serena Noceti*

*Reforming the Church* outlines the implications of an integral reform in a synodal Church.

978-0-8091-5659-7     $18.95

Other Books Published by Paulist Press

# Marian Approaches to Synodality
*Josephine Lombardi*

**FOREWORD BY**
Sr. Nathalie Becquart, XMCJ

This book explores the theme of the Synod on Synodality, "For a Synodal Church: Communion, Participation, Mission," providing an overview of the main documents of the synodal process from a Marian perspective and a vision rooted in Vatican II. Mary, "she who knows the way," shows us how to accompany others, foster greater communion and participation, and renew our focus on our baptismal mission.

978-0-8091-5670-2    $22.95

www.ingramcontent.com/pod-product-compliance
Lightning Source LLC
Chambersburg PA
CBHW070553160426
**43199CB00014B/2480**